# Walls Came Tumbling Tumbling Tumbling Tumbling Down

Michael Haley

# Walls Came Tumbling Down

## Introduction

### What's it all about?

As far as I can remember I started assembling compilations of my written work in September 2014, pulling together items from here, there and everywhere.
The 1st Volume titled "Turning Over Stones" which charted both a biography and a writing history from 1949 up to August,1998 was published in 2016.
Then volume 2, "Tall Words on a Wall" covered the period from1998 to 2004 and was published in.2020.
Hopefully you have already read and enjoyed these two?

So this is volume 3, "Walls Came Tumbling Down", which was planned to be a writing history from 2004 to the "present day". However, the project has taken so long that the "present day" has moved substantially forwards in time. This was in part due to diverting myself into other writing projects.
There were two novels which were subsequently published in between the previous 2 volumes of the compilation.
They were "The Old Dog and Duck Chronicles", a humorous look at the ramblings of two old men meeting regularly in their favourite pub which was published in 2021.
I then wrote a Whodunnit entitled "Tangles, Twists and Turns" which was published in 2022.
Originally the title, "Walls Came Tumbling Down" just seemed at a moment in time to be an appropriate one for what was happening in the world and in my life from 2004 onwards.
Eventually it also began to relate to a change in my circumstances and my spiritual understanding. Consequently there is a great deal of religious content in this work.
But after about 8 years of my "Jesus period", during which I wrote quite a large number of Christianity related songs, I became disillusioned with this spiritual direction. This was mainly due to the holier than thou attitude of many people in the church.
I left and became a born again atheist.
So although I personally needed the religious crutch for a definite

period, I eventually discovered that it no longer satisfied my needs. Religion was making me miserable and lonely, and it took me some time to realise that and to struggle free.
Nevertheless, “Walls Come Tumbling Down” illustrates a new phase of my writing life and I think some of my best work comes out of that change. Perhaps now the title would also derive from the assumption that I would eventually be released from the enjoyable but time consuming task of documenting my complete writing history in the just 3 volumes.
Best laid plans and all that!

The process of getting to volume 3 also resulted in a much greater collection of writings, and therefore, there will now be a volume 4 in this series which carries the title “Poetry, Stories, Geology and Finally”.
So that means that volume 3, “Walls Come Tumbling Down” now covers the period from 2004 to early 2018.
There will be a lot more to come in this and the next volume covering poems, songs, stories and recording history up to the present time whenever that may happen to be.
All of the writings illustrate what was on my mind at the times, and colour in moods, ups and downs, topical and personal events, and also chart my recording history. As usual, I have tried throughout the compilation to put each individual item in context with a short introductory sentence or paragraph so that you can sense where I'm coming from.
Maybe all these collections are biographies or maybe chronologies.
Maybe they are a bit of both?
Only you can decide.
Thanks for coming back for more
Enjoy!

# CHAPTER 1

## Raging Fire

***"A raging fire always burns, flames soaring strong and high,***
***A passion wild and living free, this fire, can never die."***

## If my lips could learn

***Obviously a love song, written at a special time.***

2nd July, 2004

If all the stars in the Milky Way,
Were mine to do with as I please,
My Love, I would give them all away,
Just to look into your face, and see,
Your eyes ablaze with love for me.
And if my lips could learn,
Sweet words so true,
I could say no more,
Than these short few.
Just to say " I love you".

If every tiny grain of sand,
Cried I love you a thousand ways,
I would let them all slip through my hand,
Just to wrap you in my arms and say,
How much more I love you everyday.
And if my lips could learn,
Sweet words so true,
I could say no more,
Than these short few.
Just to say " I love you".

If every wave on every sea,
Could wash your heart with love so deep,
A storm, so long, and wild, and free,
For all eternity would keep,
You safe when you are fast asleep.
And if my lips could learn,
Sweet words so true,
I could say no more,
Than these short few. Just to say " I love you".

Recording of CD album Wooden Bridge

***Recorded at Amber Sound and Light in July 2004. A selection of emotional songs including a cover of a Donovan song.***

July 2004

| Key | Song Title | WRITTEN |
|---|---|---|
| Bb (G) | Wooden Bridge | 18th May, 2004 |
| C (O) | Tuesday Universe | June, 2004 |
| A (G) | Tall Words on a Wall | 6th June, 2004 |
| D (C) | Come and Be Mine | 22nd January, 2003 |
| Eb (D) | Turquoise | Cover of a song by Donovan |
| D (C) | If my Lips could Learn | 2nd July, 2004 |

Back home soon

***I wrote these lyrics in the Garden of the Hotel Beau Rivage in Baveno on Lake Maggiore. I was missing someone.***

24th July, 2004, Lake Maggiore, Italy

Distance grows no limits,
Builds no walls, no walls to hold our hearts,
Space separates, and hesitates,
Across long days, long days when we're apart,
But lingering thoughts surround us,
Sing echoes caught to bind us from afar,
And memories will find us,
Remembering just how much in love we are.

Soon this will be over,
And I'll be coming home, back home to you.

Time makes our ragged jailor,
Holds the keys, the keys to unlock our hearts,
Imprisoned by the hours,
Across long days, long days when we're apart,
But tiny steps will gather,
Fill the void and bring us back together,
Rushing like a waterfall,
And sweeping us away on a mighty river.

Soon this will be over,
And I'll be coming home, back home to you.

## Heart's Delight

***Some of the ideas and lyrics for this song date back to the mid 1970's. The first four lines of each verse were written then. But the chorus was added in 2004. There is some influence from a song by the Irish band, the Saw Doctors. All right I stole some of their lines.***

26th September, 2004

Were there to be but one red rose,
To drink the early morning dew,
I'd stand upon the summer's edge, my love,
And steal that precious bloom for you.
You are my darlin', my heart's delight,
You are the sweet thing I'll be stayin' with tonight,
And in the mornin', when darkness ends,
You know you're gonna wake up sleepin', in my arms again,
You know you're gonna wake up sleepin', in my arms again.

Were there to but one blue sky,
To see all summer sunshine through,
I'd hover on that heaven's edge, my love,
And save that one true blue for you.
You are my darlin', my heart's delight,
You are the sweet thing I'll be stayin' with tonight,
And in the mornin', when darkness ends,
You know you're gonna wake up sleepin', in my arms again,
You know you're gonna wake up sleepin', in my arms again

Shouldn't there be just one true love,
To last for all eternity,
It's got to be, you are the one,
Someday for sure we we're gonna be.
You are my darlin', my heart's delight,
You are the sweet thing I'll be stayin' with tonight,
And in the mornin', when darkness ends,
You know you're gonna wake up sleepin', in my arms again,
You know you're gonna wake up sleepin', in my arms again

Recording of CD album of songs with words written by pupils at Writtle Junior School

***In March 2005, I did some work for the Writtle Junior School, working with pupils in year 4 and 5. The idea was that I give a talk on song-writing, and then the children write some poetry which I would attempt to set to music. The project was so successful that a few weeks later the kids were taken to Amber Sound and Light recording studios, and the songs were recorded. CD albums produced from that recording were sold by the school, and all proceeds went to the school funds."***

March 2005

| Key | Song Title | WRITTEN |
|---|---|---|
| D (C2) | Still a Mystery | OCT 2004 |
| Bb(C3) | Fruit Squash | OCT 2004 |
| A (C2) | Without You | OCT 2004 |
| D (C2) | Woodworm Kiss | 26th November, 2003 |
| Am(O) | Come Fly Together | OCT 2004 |
| D (C2) | Mr Taylor | OCT 2004 |
| A (C2) | Talking Trousers | 13th August, 2003 |
| G (O) | Play these Songs Please | OCT 2004 |
| C (O) | Teachers | OCT 2004 |
| G (O) | Walking talkin Snowman | OCT 2004 |
| C (O) | A Mystery Unknown | OCT 2004 |
| G (O) | The Ferret Song | OCT 2004 |

## Raging Fire

***Just another painful and heartfelt love song.***

9th October, 2005

You will never know how many turning leaves fall
from the damp autumn forest trees.
You will never know how many grassy blades sway
in the green lazy meadow breeze.
You will never know how many distant stars fill
the vast empty evening skies.
You will never see all the floods of tears
in a broken hearted lover's eyes.

You'll never have enough love
no matter how hard you try;
You'll never have enough between
your hallos and goodbyes;
You'll never be contented
to have less than you desire,
And what you give back in return
must burn, burn, burn,
Like a raging fire.

A raging fire always burns;
flames soaring strong and high;
A passion wild and living free –
this fire can never die.

You will always walk beside
green meadows and cool streams,
While falling leaves forever fill
the forests of your dreams,
But keep your eyes turned up to heaven
and reach out for the stars,
And when your tears subside
you'll find out who you are.

You'll never have enough love
no matter how hard you try;

You'll never have enough between
your hallos and goodbyes;
You'll never be contented
to have less than you desire,
And what you give back in return,
must burn, burn, burn,
Like a raging fire.

A raging fire always burns;
flames soaring strong and high;
A passion wild and living free –
this fire can never die.

Recording of CD album Separate Heavens

***A selection of love songs recorded at Amber Sound and Light.***

16th November, 2005

| Key | | Song Title | WRITTEN |
|---|---|---|---|
| G | (O) | Heart's Delight | 26th September, 2004 |
| A | (G) | Separate Heavens | 21st April, 2004 |
| G | (O) | Back Home Soon | 24th July, 2004 |
| Bm | (O) | Raging Fire | 9th October, 2005 |

Lost Child

***I was in church one Sunday morning a small child was crying in the row immediately in front of me and as I closed my eyes to praise the Lord, a vision came to me. I saw a child crying, abandoned on a beach at the end of a summer seaside day. But this lost child did not stay desperate and alone for long. After a short while I heard the sounds of Mum and Dad comforting her and carrying her away to safety. The thought stayed in my mind, and later that same day this poem came out.***

8th January, 2006

In the pale yellow light
of a long seaside evening
On a nearly empty beach
as a fading sunset dies,
Among the salty tasting tang
of dampening sea breezes,
There calls an eerie, lonely sound
that pulls my urgent gaze.

Under the lazy swoop and swirl
of searching seagull glides,
Blurring at the darkened edge
of softly lapping waves,
Along a sandy twilight waterline I faintly spy,
A lost child, solitary,
crying by the sea.

Tears are smothered in the swell,
cries are muted by the sounds,
She stands up and looks around,
there's no one to be seen,
No one to be seen, no one to be seen.

Where are you my child?
My Child where are you?
Where are you my child?
My Child where are you?

Where are you my child?
My Child where are you?
Where are you my child?
My Child where are you?

And as the ever moving hand
of dark relentless night,
Sweeps away the last few rays
of summer's dying light,
A growing mass of deepening shadows
swallows up the sound,
And carries her away to be
in the warmth of welcome arms.

Tears are smothered in the swell,
cries are muted by the sounds,
She was lost, but now she's found,
on her way back home,
On her way back home, on her way back home.

Bright day is soon abandoned to
cool night's persuading charms,
Her failing soft hold now releases,
crying ceases, she is safe,
And all remains in stillness
are the gently lapping waves,
In worship to the restless spirits
of creation and always.

Tears are smothered in the swell,
cries are muted by the sounds,
She was lost, but now she's found,
she's on her way back home,
And all remains in stillness
are the gently lapping waves,
In worship to the restless spirits
of creation and always.

Heaven in your dreams

***By now you may be getting quite sick of my love songs. Tough! Here's another one. The poem referred to in the first verse just happens to be one I wrote. The line in a song, in the second verse is from the ELO number 'Hold on Tight to Your Dream'.***

9th April, 2006

There's a line in a poem,
and I remember what it said,
'By the time I reach Heaven,
I will probably be dead',
And when I first thought about it,
I'm not sure I understood,
Whether what the writer said,
could be bad or could be good,
Then one day our lives changed forever,
and I knew how much words were worth,
Cause suddenly, it seemed to be,
that we had Heaven here on Earth.

Be good, be safe, be mine,
And carry my heart there on your sleeve,
Dream all our dreams in Heaven, my love,
See Heaven in our dreams.

There's a line in song, ringing true,
or so it seems,
It says 'All you've gotta do is,
hold on tight to your dreams',
And I often think about it,
and I'm so sure I understand,
That what the song is saying is,
our future's in our hands,
All our lives in constant change,
shifting sands and rolling seas,
So let's hold on tight together,
so you can dream a dream with me.

Hideaway

***Perhaps now you would be wondering if things were starting to go wrong somewhere along the way?***

5th September, 2006

You and me alone; surrounded, surrendered,
To a star-strewn summer sky;
Where the pearl moon, glowing,
Lights the swirling waters flowing, to the distance,
where the shimmering,
Orange city lights are blurring far away on the horizon.
So shall we begin to count the stars together?
Only knowing it's going to take us till forever?
We can stay here. We can play here.
You and me alone; surrounded, surrendered -
Free lost souls in a star-strewn summer sky.

Don't leave me here alone!
It's taken so long, so long to find you;
I want to hide away, hide away inside your heart.
Here is where you belong!
Come let me hide away,
hide away inside your heart.

You and me alone; surrounded, surrendered,
To a wind-blown midnight sea;
Wild wind, untamed, blowing,
From our high place, overflowing i
n the distance, disappearing,
where the sea and sky are joining,
watery hands on the horizon.
So shall we begin to count the waves together?
Only knowing it's going to take us till forever?
We can stay here. We can play here.
You and me again; surrounded, surrendered -
Free lost souls in a wind-blown midnight sea.

Don't leave me here alone!
It's taken so long, so long to find you;
I want to hide away, hide away inside your heart.
Here is where you belong!
Come let me hide away,
hide away inside your heart.

Thoughts on Love

***Reflective thoughts.***

11th November, 2006

When offered in truth from the very heart of being,
the words "I love you"
cannot be weakened or diminished by time,
nor adversity, nor the frequency
with which they are spoken

12th November, 2006

Indeed, whilst the words "I love you"
are by themselves supremely powerful,
it is love itself that is indisputably strengthened
and enlarged by the passage of time,
the experiences of adversity,
and the frequency of its revelation.

## Storehouse of Memories

***Your brain is a storehouse of memories collected***
***as you move from place to place and time to time.***
***We store both pleasurable and painful memories,***
***and sometimes it feels like the storehouse is overflowing.***
***There is no pain as acute as the break-up of a relationship.***

10th April, 2007

I have collected a storehouse of memories,
As bold billowed sails of a galleon may gather far winds,
Harnessed, to sail from place to place, and time to time,
Sometimes becalmed in the doldrums
and moved to silence.
Other times raging and violent at the mercy of a storm,
Or waiting In the soft eye of a hurricane,
Or riding on the tall crest of a wave,
And praying to be saved.

My storehouse is filled to its brim, overflowing,
A Universe vast and infinite, expanding and growing,
Ever moving, never still for long,
And never knowing where or when it's going to end.

And when searching my storehouse of memories,
I'm hovering on great slow gliding wings,
Above empty endless expanses of open blue ocean,
And so, I look, I look, I look for love,
And have never found it as I have in you.

Maybe I'm just David, Bathsheba is my aim,
Maybe I'm a saint who keeps a dragon in a cave,
Maybe I'm just King Canute, trying to hold back the waves,
Maybe, Oh Maybe, all those broken Hallelujahs
could not save me,
Maybe, Oh Maybe, I love you,
and that was all I needed to say.

My storehouse still has room
for all the words left unsaid,
And no promises spoke would be broken,
But still I could sense when you
were slipping away, from me,
Like the drift, in the depths,
of a calm quiet ocean.

Honywood Oak

***The Honywood Oak is an 800 year old tree in the wonderfully manicured Marks Hall Gardens and Arboretum near Coggeshall.***
***I've visited this beautiful park many times, and on a sunny day it's a great place to breathe in the air and feel good to be alive.***
***The Honywood Oak is protected and you're not supposed to touch it. But how often do you get a chance to touch a living thing that's 800 years old? What did the world look and feel like when this magnificent tree was just an acorn? If the tree could speak what marvellous stories would it have to tell? The urge to break the rules was irresistible!"***

12th August, 2007

As two children, in a nearly empty but welcoming playground, We explore and make adventure, among the whispering boughs, and rustling leaves, Soft damp grass beneath our feet, perfect mirror skies above our heads ,And fairy nymphs flitting through the sunbeams, Watching as we smile and enjoy being together.

Beside the placid looking-glass lake, and gently lapping waterfalls, Uncovering the aromatic secrets in the seclusion of a high-walled garden, Absorbing the luscious coolness of the fern-frond shade ,And listening across the meadow green, To the excited chatter of a wedding party

As we marvel at the history hiding canopy of a tree as old as time, A silent watching witness to the passage of the years, Gathering seasons and yearning for the freedom of the skies above, Through white snows, in spring buds, in summer proud and abundant, And in autumn changing as the myriad of colours falls and dies.

To touch this miracle, we two children of the Universe,
Are at one with the tree's perseverance, and our transience,
But we have here tried to understand how it feels to be so close to God.

# CHAPTER 2

## Wicked Angels, Luscious Demons

***"Dark whispers keep my mind at bay,***
***The jungle hills drum far away,***
***But in sweet rustle autumn golds,***
***Under wide lonely skies unfold."***

Return to the Wooden Bridge

***In May 2004 I wrote a very personal song for someone special. That song was called "Wooden Bridge". Some phrases from the original are included again - "time balanced on a ridge", "cascading through the shade" "a garden perfect made" This poem is both a reminiscence and a lament for a relationship that had finished, but still hurt enormously."***

11th April, 2009

When the guardian angels sit waiting by the kissing gates,
Whispering their secrets, their secrets about us,
And the tall trees reveal their truths to tell tales,
Of how, and why, and where, and when we became lovers,
Then we'll return,
To where time balanced on a ridge,
And hold each other oh so close once again,
Face to face, eyes to smiling eyes,
Lips to lips, Heart to burning heart,
Upon a wooden bridge.

Where we two children of the Universe, held the world spellbound,
Stood cascading, cascading through the shade,
For the moment we steal, the sweetest of kisses
Still innocent but knowing, in a garden perfect made,
Then we'll relive,
When love moved us to the edge,
And feel that simmering passion once again,
Face to face, eyes to smiling eyes,
Lips to lips, heart to burning heart,
Upon our wooden bridge.

So many, oh so many special times and places,
But just one,
Where we first knew,
Where we first understood,
Where we were first, and last, and only.

## I'm scared

***Written as a song with a slow blues format.***
***I always felt it was incomplete until I found the 3rd verse after a nine and a half year search. The subject is loneliness, with an acidic theme of "I know what's going on here, and I am well aware that I'm being used."***
***Was recorded in November 2000, obviously at that time minus the 3rd verse.***

3rd June, 2000, 3rd verse added 23rd December, 2009

I've been here, I've been there,
I've been out in the cold,
Been a slave to your wishes,
I've been bought, I've been sold,
It was hard to realise,
It was all just a game,
There was pain in the truth babe,
And then the tears came.
And it feels like, you never really loved me,
It feels like, you never ever cared,
It feels like, you're as cold as ice babe,
You got me scared, I'm really scared.

You just took me for granted,
Fooled me all along,
So that I'd be disappointed,
Like in some sad old love song,
You played with my heart,
And you messed up my mind,
And I can't understand babe,
How could you be so unkind.
And it feels like, you never really loved me,
It feels like, you never ever cared,
It feels like, you're as cold as ice babe,
You got me scared, I'm really scared.

And so every man is an island,
And every woman the sea,
Just like a tsunami,
You overwhelmed me,
And now I'm washed up as driftwood,
My heart's so battered and bruised,
I'm useless, I'm worthless, I'm no good,
I've been dazed and confused for so long its not true,
And it feels like, you never really loved me,
It feels like, you never ever cared,
It feels like, you're as cold as ice babe,
You got me scared, I'm really scared. I'm so scared.

## Last song for you

***This is exactly what it says on the tin.***
***A last song for someone special.***

29th September/19th October, 2011

Not so long ago and certainly not so far away;
Out of the blue, suddenly,
I found myself falling in love with you.

You were beautiful; sunsets for my eyes.
You were magical; music to my ears.
You were dangerous; I was hypnotised.
You were the one.

Your voice was like a whisper in the wilderness.
Your words they fell together like the rain.
I climbed aboard your runaway train and held on for the ride;
So tired of playin' hide and seek to cover up the pain -
Longin' for a time when you'd be only mine again.

You were beautiful; sunsets for my eyes.
You were magical; music to my ears.
You were dangerous; I was hypnotised.
You were the one.

But bitter sweet became the theme tune for our songs.
Mixed fortune stole the scenes for our refrain.
We'd fallen from the ladder that climbed up to the stars.
A loaded dice had fated us to lose our loving game.
No chance would be awaiting us to stop the breaking chain.

You were beautiful; sunsets for my eyes.
You were magical; music to my ears.
You were dangerous; I was hypnotised.
You were the one.

Your footsteps always danced so soft across my heart.
Tiptoed a rainbow's edge to steal my soul.
When elusive tastes of ecstasy became forbidden fruit,

Be sure that I was never blind to the precious dreams you hold,
And never mind I still love you with a heart of pure gold.

You were beautiful; sunsets for my eyes.
You were magical; music to my ears.
You were dangerous; I was hypnotised.
You were the one.

Now no longer here, disappeared, so far far away -
Now I know, it so clear, this will be the last song for you.

Muddy Waters (Electric Bluesman)

***Perhaps now is a good time to change the mood with a song That is about something to do with music rather than love. If you like music, and you really like blues and bluesmen, then Muddy Waters must come somewhere near the top of a very long list which might include Robert Johnson and Big Bill Broonzy?***
***The song had remained unrecorded for a long time until it featured on an album I called "And the band played on", recorded at Highfield Studios in November 2015.***

8th November, 2011, amended 17th June, 2015

Don't wanna go to Mississippi
to see no levee break,
Don't wanna go to New York City
to climb the Empire State,
Don't wanna go walking with my baby
by the San Francisco Bay,
Don't wanna go to Augusta Georgia
to see no Masters play,
No Way Tiger Woods, even if I could!
But I'd drive from L.A. on Route 66,
goin' eastward all the way,
With my destination Chicago,
to see where Muddy Waters played,
See where Muddy Waters played.

I'm not gonna go down by the riverside
to see the Grand Coulee dam,
I'm not gonna go to Las Vegas,
I ain't no gamblin' man,
I'm not gonna go to Orlando
to see no Disney World,
I'm not gonna go to the west coast
to flirt with California girls,
Best in the world are English girls!
But I'd drive from L.A. on Route 66,
with my pedal down all the way,
Heading for the city of Chicago,

to see where Muddy Waters played,
See where Muddy Waters played.

You can't make me go to the Grand Canyon
to look at no hole in the ground,
You can't make me go to Detroit t
o hear that Tamla Motown sound,
You can't make me go to Graceland
to see where Elvis lived and died,
You can't make me go to Watergate
to see where Nixon lied,
And lied, and lied, and lied, and lied!
But I'd drive from L.A. on Route 66,
with my radio on all the way,
Making a beeline for Chicago,
to be where Muddy Waters played,
Be where Muddy Waters played.

I ain't gonna go to Nashville
to get no country music twang,
I ain't gonna go to Woodstock t
o be where the hippies sang,
I ain't gonna go to Niagara
to watch the water flow,
I ain't gonna go to the Alamo
to watch a Texas rodeo,
Yee Har! Aw Shucks! Yippee- yi-oh!
But I'd drive from L.A. on Route 66,
goin' hell for leather all the way,
Bound for the city of Chicago,
to be where Muddy Waters played,
Be where Muddy Waters played.

Why should I go to Hollywood
to movie star fantasy land,
Why should I go to New Orleans
for the Dixieland jazz bands,
Why should I go to Indianapolis
to see no five hundred mile race,
Why should I go to Oklahoma
to join in a tornado chase,

Too windy, I'm just too windy!
But one day I'll drive on Route 66,
goin' eastward from L.A.,
Just so I can be in Chicago,
in the city where Muddy Waters played,
In the city where Muddy Waters played.

## Remember Road

***Remember Road is filled with my boyhood reminiscence. It's all memories, both topical for the time and personal. The talking blues format allows me to be documentary in each verse. and then make ad hoc commentary from my own recollections.***

22nd November, 2011

Let me take you for a stroll down Remember Road,
And a walk across Nostalgia Square,
For a winding wander down Memory Lane,
To pick my forget-me-nots there.

Do you remember when Christmas didn't start
in September, just after the Summer return,
When Bonfire night was just one night,
for everybody's big bang and big burn,
We'd hardly heard of Halloween,
there was no Trick or Treat,
And nobody needed to be frightened at night,
when walking down the street?

Back in the days when Christmas came in December,
we had a real tree with candles to light,
There were strange smells like tangerines and chocolate,
and they arrived on Christmas Eve night,
Back then Christmas dinner was just chicken,
and everyone enjoyed the sprouts (twice!),
And when I loosened a tooth on the sixpence
in the Christmas pudding, the tooth fairy still came out.

When I was 6, I had my first taste of stardom,
when I was in the school nativity play,
I was 1 of the 3 little shepherds,
dressed in orange crepe paper outfits,
Suddenly, just before Jesus was born,
the shepherds were standing in puddle,
After somebody accidentally pee'd them self on stage.,
You've guessed it, Yes! It was me!

Let me take you for a stroll down Remember Road,
And a walk across Nostalgia Square,
For a winding wander down Memory Lane,
To pick my forget-me-nots there.

Do you recall, when we all had to walk to school,
and the cardboard in our shoes was getting wet,
When there was free school milk in the morning,
and school dinners were the best meal you'd get,
When we learned our 12-times table from a blackboard,
and went home covered in chalk dust,
Were you around when we had pounds,
shillings and pence,
and it made good sense to us?

When you slept in a bed made with sheets and blankets,
and if it was very cold your Dad's overcoat as well,
We only had a fireplace in the living room,
do you remember that cosy glow and coal fire smell,
We still went to school in the winter snows,
never mind the weather, and no matter what,
You shared the bath water with the whole family,
once a week whether you needed it or not.

Because I had 4 sisters
I always went into the bath last of all,
well, I was outnumbered by them
The water was cold and mucky by then,
sometimes I came out more dirty than when I went in,
Especially in the summer when I'd fallen in the river,
that happened at least twice a week.
I always got the blame
for the dirty ring around the bath,
what a bloody cheek,

Let me take you for a stroll down Remember Road,
And a walk across Nostalgia Square,
For a winding wander down Memory Lane,
To pick my forget-me-nots there.

We might go scrumping for apples,
play Knock down Ginger,
or a million other pranks and tricks,
We'd go to Saturday Morning Pictures,
or sneak into Woolworth's to nick the pick-n-mix.
The Barbershop was in the back
of Finlay's tobacconist,
short back-and-sides the only choice,
Because Sir might want
"something for the weekend",
women weren't allowed in with the boys.

What a treat to go Southend on a steam train,
excitement rising as the sea drew near,
We had bags of chips, candyfloss,
watched Punch and Judy,
and walked to the end of the pier,
For hours long we played happily
in the sewage outfall,
and ate sandwiches made by Mum's fair hand,
Went home contented
with seaweed between our toes,
and pockets full of shells and sand.

Once a year we went to the Southend at night time,
when they switched the illuminations on,
In those days there was a magical place,
up on the cliffs called Never, Never Land,
A fantasy land filled with fairy lights,
and cartoon characters, and little waterfalls,
I loved it so much I wanted to live there,
and often refused to go home.

Let me take you for a stroll down Remember Road,
And a walk across Nostalgia Square,
For a winding wander down Memory Lane,
To pick my forget-me-nots there.

There were so little traffic around in the street,
you could safely play football, cricket, or tennis,
Indoors we played Ludo,

Snakes and Ladders, Tiddlywinks,
we were Beryl the Peril, or Dennis the Menace,
We all had manners, said please and thank you,
excuse me, and I'm sorry, and all with a smile,
And Father Christmas didn't have to be CRB checked,
to make sure he wasn't a paedophile.

On Sundays we listened to the radio,
there was Family Favourites,
and the Billy Cotton Band Show,
On the monochrome 9 inch telly
we watched Robin Hood,
and Roger Moore was Ivanhoe,
The whole house was filled with a lovely smell,
as Mum baked cakes in the afternoon,
And all us kids hung around expectantly,
and argued about who was going to lick the bowl.

So its certain my friends, that life was
surely much simpler then,
Even  if our table was bare,
There were no CDs, or DVDs, or LCD TVs,
No  IPODs, or mobile phones back there ,
We communicated by stopping and talking face to face,
everyone had time to listen,
There was a gazunder under the bed,
we were lucky 'cause we did have a pot to piss in.

There was no Facebook, No Twitter, No Email,
No Internet, No XBOX, No Ebay,
No Google, and certainly no pot noodle,
No political correctness, Thank God!
No money, scruffy clothes, no cars, a snotty nose,
no sweets, not very much too eat,
But there was lots of love, and lots of fun,
and smiles from everyone.

Well we went for a stroll down Remember Road,
And a walk across Nostalgia Square,
For a winding wander down Memory Lane,
To pick my forget-me-nots there.

Wicked Angels, Luscious Demons

***While on a Creative Writing Course the inspiration for the first verse of this poem arrived during an in-class exercise stemming from the two words "Dark Whispers". A few hours later I had written the other two verses, and a day later the "Wicked Angels, Luscious Demons, flying round, in my dreams." idea was added. The poem is perfectly formatted to become a song, and was recorded on the CD album "Dangerous Curves." at Highfield Studios.***

1st to 3rd December,2011

Dark whispers keep my mind at bay,
The jungle hills drum far away,
But in sweet rustle autumn golds,
Under wide lonely skies unfold.

Oh peace to keep my mind at rest,
And fill the place I love the best,
The glorious sun, brilliant undimmed,
A balmy breeze, not biting wind.

For chasing angels through the haze,
My ransom's paid for summer days,
Wicked Angels, Luscious Demons,
Flying round, in my dreams.

The silent slip of twilight's hand,
Goes sliding smooth across this land,
And rides disguised into the dawn,
To break the night spell so forlorn.

Oh peace to keep my heart full-blessed,
And steal the time I love the best,
The moon's cool shadows wait unspent,
To wonder why and where we went.

Just chasing angels through the crowds,
And painting rainbows on the clouds,
Wicked Angels, Luscious Demons,
Flying round, in my dreams.

Whilst mail trains thunder through the night,
To cities blazed in neon light,
We sleep entwined and face to face,
Together locked in soft embrace.

At peace to keep our hearts on song,
On Heaven's edge where we belong,
And lost in dreams the Sandman brings,
On gentle glides of angel's wings.
We chase our whispers through 'til morn,
When night's dark curtain shroud is gone,
Wicked Angels, Luscious Demons,
Flying round, in my dreams.

Swinging Sixties Talking Blues

**I'd thought long and hard about what to write for the Creative Writing Course homework supposed to be entitled "The Doors Project" I abandoned previous plans for what I hoped would be a safe option. I was conscious that I was on the course for a different reason to the rest of the course attendees. (to write lyrics for songs)**
**My Remember Road Talking Blues had been well received, and so I thought I'd stick to a successful formula. So I came up with another talking blues called" Swinging Sixties Talking Blues".**
**The verses are standard 4 line poetry rhyming couplets, and the ad hoc comments are free form. Perhaps it's another history lesson, or maybe it's once again the ramblings of somebody living in the past. You can decide.**
**I hope you like it It starts with an easy chorus, and takes off from there with a verse for each year in the 60's.**

21st December, 2011 to 4th January, 2012

Welcome to the swinging sixties,
some of my halcyon days,
Though it was oh so long ago,
it still seems like yesterday.

In 1961,
The Russians sent a man into space,
Yuri Gagarin he was called,
In April just for fun, strapped into Vostok1,
he spun around the world,
Then the Berlin Wall appeared overnight,
With guns and dogs installed,
And the free world stood there helpless,
and watched the Iron Curtain fall.

Meanwhile back in Merrie England:
I listened to Radio Luxembourg
on my new transistor radio
made in Hong Kong, and managed to pass the 13+
And read the Lion the Witch and the Wardrobe.

That year Elvis was King, Ah ha ha!
Elisabeth was Queen,
And Gay still meant cheerful and brightly coloured.

Welcome to the swinging sixties,
some of my halcyon days,
Though it was oh so long ago,
it still seems like yesterday.

In 1962,
The Russians shipped missiles to Cuba,
And the Yanks went to action stations,
As Khrushchev banged his shoe on the desk
defying the United Nations,
We held our breath, as certain death,
Spelled the end of civilisation,
But President Kennedy saved the world from nuclear annihilation.

So the world wasn't saved by a Bruce Willis, Arnold Schwarzenegger, John Wayne or Superman type of character,
Well, Khrushchev was a vodka swilling, erratic, WW2 hero,
And Kennedy was allegedly a womaniser,
having an affair with Marilyn Monroe among others.
Perhaps the moral is, its better to be a lover than a fighter?
If you want to save the world that is!

Welcome to the swinging sixties,
some of my halcyon days,
Though it was oh so long ago,
it still seems like yesterday.

In 1963,
Valentina Tereshkova became the first woman in space,
The Beatles 'Please, please me' was released,
As Christine Keeler and Mandy Rice Davies
brought our government to its knees,
Bob Dylan told us the times are a-changin',
James Bond came from Russia with love,
In November in Dallas John Kennedy
went to meet the angels above.

Meanwhile in high school wearing
a school uniform3 sizes too big.
You know, turn ups of industrial strength
on both the trousers and blazer,
In English Lit: I was reading a boring book
called Mr Polly by H. G.. Wells.
Soon abandoned for; The Gun by C S Forrester,
and Allan Quartermain by Rider Haggard.
When not studying English Lit
I read Lady Chatterley's Lover,
As a result I became so depraved
I joined the Woodpecker darts team,
started smoking and drinking, and completely forgot
where I was when Kennedy was assassinated.

Welcome to the swinging sixties,
some of my halcyon days,
Though it was oh so long ago,
it still seems like yesterday.

In 1964,
This was the year all the oldies groaned,
They didn't understand the words
Of the Beatles and the Stones,
'The weekend starts here', they said
On Ready, Steady, Go,
And all the in-crowd tuned in
to Caroline on pirate radio.

Meanwhile, here in still Great Britain:
I could moo-oo-oo-oo-oove like Jagger
James Bond was in Goldfinger, Shirley Bassey sang it,
and Harold Wilson became Prime Minister
He was obsessed with the pound in your pocket,
and the price of pipe tobacco.

My headmaster Mr Harry told me
he didn't like my Beatles hairstyle.
I said that's OK 'cause I didn't like
what was left of his hair.

He sent a letter home to my mum about it.
She wrote back saying she failed to see
how the length of my hair could affect my academic ability.

I gave up smoking, and soon after
passed 10 GCE 'O' levels .
Mum was delighted, Mr Harry was outraged,
and refused to present me with my certificates.

Welcome to the swinging sixties,
some of my halcyon days,
Though it was oh so long ago,
it still seems like yesterday.

In 1965,
On the only 3 TV channels, still monochrome,
comedy and satire were rife,
There was Not so much a programme
more a way of life,
That was the week that was, better known as TW3,
And Not only but also
with Peter Cook and cuddly Dudley.

Meanwhile, in a quiet world for Russians:
The media discovered Mods and Rockers ,
I went into the 6th form, got bored bored bored with it,
And discovered girls.

Janet Robinson was my first girlfriend,
Her dad ran the local chippie,
and 10 minutes of snogging with
Janet Fishshop as she was known,
made you smell like last night's haddock and chips.
Oh! I gave up smoking again
and took up eating fish and chips!

Welcome to the swinging sixties,
some of my halcyon days,
Though it was oh so long ago,
it still seems like yesterday.

In 1966,
If you were a dedicated follower of fashion,
You bought your clothes in Carnaby Street,
The Monkees arrived on our TV's
as America's answer to the Beatles,
Mary Quant and Twiggy promoted the mini skirt,
The World Cup was in England,
and was won by players from West Ham,
And President Lyndon B Johnson delighted
in napalming Vietnam.

Meanwhile,
I left School, started work in London,
bought a Lambretta scooter and became a mod.
I had to leave school because
the uniform was 3 sizes too small,
trousers, now turn-up-less (A new word )
and flapping round my knees,
And a blazer with sleeves on my worn out elbows.
Got drunk for the first time
the night after West Ham won the World Cup.
Good Excuse!
And girls discovered me.
Well! It was the era of the Mini skirt,
Women's lib and burning bras,
and most important of all deodorants for men.
Old Spice and Avon Spicy. Mmm!

Welcome to the swinging sixties,
some of my halcyon days,
Though it was oh so long ago,
it still seems like yesterday.

In 1967,
It was all Waterloo sunsets in the summer of Love,
JImi Hendrix and Purple Haze,
Hippies, and flower power, and San Francisco
filling those heady days,
Experiments with colour TV,
And the first heart transplants underway,

And in a time of psychedelia
did anybody really see Emily play?

Meanwhile, it wasn't all good,
The Torrey Canyon spilled thousands of tons of oil
all over Cornwall's beaches,
and was bombed by the RAF,
I gave up smoking, and met, loved
and lost Denise Frost,
my first serious girlfriend.
The Israelis had a 6-day war
and petrol prices rose to about 1/6 a gallon,
I tell you times were really hard!

I have to point out that after 50 years
I still don't know what a halcyon is?
And I'm convinced that if I ever found out,
I probably wouldn't be able to afford one!

That's actually a complete fib, I looked it up,
and the halcyon is a mythical bird akin to a kingfisher.
So there! Isn't education a wonderful thing?
and Wikipedia!

Welcome to the swinging sixties,
some of my halcyon days,
Though it was oh so long ago,
it still seems like yesterday.

In 1968,
It was the year of protest marches,
And we shall overcome,
Of CND, and Ban the Bomb, and anti-Vietnam,
Martin Luther King was inspired to have a dream,
And was then assassinated,
Dubcek gave the Czechoslovaks hope,
and so the Russians invaded.

Meanwhile,
I bought a guitar, and learned a few Bob Dylan songs,
Spent most Sundays marching

from Trafalgar Square to Grosvenor Square,
Watched Dads Army and Doctor Who on the telly,
still not in colour
Drank loads of Watneys Red Barrel,
Apollo8 orbited the moon,
and I overcame the urge to give up smoking.

Yeah, about this halcyon business,
when I wrote this song I thought about
saying "salad days" instead.
But then, who wants to listen to songs
about lettuce, cucumber and tomatoes?
That's not true either,
Salad days is from Shakespeare's Antony and Cleopatra,
"**Salad days**" is an idiomatic expression,
referring to a youthful time,
accompanied by the inexperience, enthusiasm, idealism,
innocence, or indiscretion
that one associates with a young person.
That sounds a bit like me!

Welcome to the swinging sixties,
some of my kingfisher days,
Though it was oh so long ago,
it still seems like yesterday.

In 1969,
We watched Apollo11 land upon the moon,
Neil Armstrong's giant leap was the first,
Let's not forget, it also made Michael Collins
the loneliest man in the Universe,
Bob Dylan came and played at Isle of Wight,
Concorde took off for its maiden flight,
And John Cleese did those silly walks
on Monty Pythons Flying Circus.

Meanwhile as the sixties drew to a close:
Most public telephone boxes were vandalised,
The pubs still closed at half past ten,
and the 3 channels on TV started about 4
and finished about 11,

And the only fast food restaurant was the Wimpy Bar.
All those pink bits on maps of the world began to disappear,
as all those ex-colonial countries renamed themselves,
usually with something starting with a Z,
and immediately started their civil war.

On the good side England swings
like a pendulum do? Eh?
You could lay in a bed warmed by your electric blanket,
Which you bought with your green shield stamps,
Stare at the TV test card, or a fascinating lava lamp,
Then wake up to a fresh cuppa courtesy of your Goblin Teas-made,
Which you bought with your Embassy coupons.
Such wealth, such decadence!
Oh! By the way, did I tell you, I gave up smoking?

Goodbye to the swinging sixties,
some of my salad days,
Though it was oh so long ago,
it still seems like yesterday.

# CHAPTER 3

## Dangerous Curves

***"Running my wheels over dangerous curves,***
***Showing my skills on dangerous curves,***
***Moving in for the kill on dangerous curves.***
***Man I'm just a petrol-head on dangerous curves."***

Delicate genius

***The song is dedicated to all those performers who sought fame, and having found it and revelled in it, they then found themselves unable to deal with the stark contrast between their stage(performance) life, and their off-stage (private) life. There are many of them, not just musicians, of which the a recent example at the time of writing was Amy Winehouse. Let's not forget among others : Brian Jones, Jim Morrison, Jimi Hendrix, Janis Joplin, Elvis Presley, Michael Hutchence etc.***
***They all contributed to our lives, and unwillingly gave theirs.***
***The song has been performed but never recorded.***

12th to 24th January, 2012

You were born for performance, made for the stage,
You're moody and marvellous, musical genius,
But the seeds of destruction were sewn, in the marrow of your bones, Because you die in the quiet, the nothing of silence.
With that broody precarious, lunatic madness,
You are walking a razor's edge, stalking dark shadows alone.

You're out on the stage, where you strut and excel,
Your heart beats so rapid, your ego it swells,
You build the excitement, climbing to a crescendo,
Songs and stories and anthems, incantations and spells.

They may love you enough to give you what you want,
But they can't give you just what you need,

In the action the zone, and laying your groove,
Suddenly once again, you're in the spotlight,
Making the sounds, that revive and excite you,
Leading your heroes, like gladiators to fight.

They may love you enough to give you what you want,
But they can't give you just what you need,

Where you're giving your all, your heart soul and tears,
Your audience captive, and at your command,
You demand their attention, they clamour for more,
Like a feeding frenzy, of faces and hands,

They may love you enough to give you what you want,
But they can't give you just what you need,

On reaching the encores, you feel its over too quickly,
As you drink in the pleasure, and then sink without trace,
It crushes your spirit, like a poisonous gas,
And the moments you treasure, disappear into space.

They may love you enough to give you what you want,
But they can't give you just what you need,

When each new day begins, in drama and shock waves,
And crash-lands in your brain, Like a grief stricken plane,
There's fast food and bourbon, and cigarette binges,
And the pusher's delights for hiding the pain.

When the dead hand of silence, falls uneasy upon you,
Though it's fingers caress, like a lover's soft touch,
You're in need of the rush, that the music will bring again,
Because the aftermath calm is never,  never enough.

There's new songs to rehearse, for a faraway venue,
But the quiet desperation, is sure to undermine
Hiding you from sensations, you're missing so much.
Before the show must go on one more time.

You were born for performance, made for the stage,
You're moody and marvellous, musical genius,
But the seeds of destruction were sewn, in the marrow of your
bones, Because you die in the quiet, the nothing of silence.
With that broody precarious, lunatic madness,
You are walking a razor's edge, stalking dark shadows alone.

***"It was only a matter of a few days after finishing this song, that Whitney Houston become yet another victim."***

Tricks with time

***A homework exercise which I turned into another reflective look at life and living. At the tender age of 63, I was wondering just how long I'm going to last, and what I might have done right or wrong along the way. This song was recorded at Highfield Studios in June 2015 on the CD album "Dangerous Curves", and abandoning the coda this became a different song called "Promises and Regrets". (see later).***

21st December, 2011 to 8th February, 2012

Well, you were naked on arrival, with nothing to bring,
But hell-bent on survival, with new songs to sing,
Growing into someone with hopes, and plans, and dreams,
When you were so very young, and the world was your pearl,
With your heart on your sleeve, your mind in a swirl,
Impatient and impetuous, as time is not what it seems.

Now most of your experience, is in the rear view mirror,
Reflections and memories, as your hair grows grey and thinner,
Now wonder's turned to wisdom, and emptiness into space,
Can you content yourself, with how you spent your days?,
Did you grow happy with your lot, or just set in your ways?,
As time became etched in, every precious line of your face.

Did you do it all for love, did you do it for art?,
Did you lead with your head, or follow your heart?,
Can you put it all down to providence or fate?,
Did you fall as a saint, or stand tall as a sinner?,
Can you live long as a loser, or die young as a winner?,
Are you a fool rushing in, or an angel who hesitates?

Remember when your life, was still way ahead of you,
And you had so many things, to look forward to,
You held no fear for the mountains you needed to climb,
Then all your days and years, went flashing by,
And some of those you love, had to say goodbye,
You found your mind was, playing tricks with time.

Tomorrows tumble ever faster,
through a trapdoor, here and now, today,
Assembling in a vault of memories, becoming yesterdays,
Yesterdays.

Creative (Song) Writing

***I set myself a challenge to write a poem featuring every one of my friends on the Creative Writing Course. First of all I gathered some information about each one, asking them to tell me what they did for a living, what were their hobbies, and interests, and something surprising or unusual about them. Once I had the poem finalised, I set about putting it to music and creating a song, which I had the privilege to play for them all. I stole the tune from a Bob Dylan classic called "Hard Rain's gonna Fall." Fits perfectly.***

15th/16th February, 2012

Oh where have you been my gullible son?,
Oh where have you been my darling young one?,
I've been to the Friary, to learn about writing,
I've been to write stories, and do some speed novelling
I've written some new songs, and played them to new people
I've spent Thursday mornings, with some friends who were strangers
And I wrote, and I sung, and I laughed, and had fun,
And I'll miss them all, when they're gone.

Oh who was your tutor my gullible son?,
Oh who was your tutor my darling young one?,
T'was someone called Maggie, taught me about writing,
She writes and she teaches, does walking and gardening,
She loves the outdoors, and the National Portrait Gallery,
She was born in Trinidad, and used to be very skinny,
She challenged her cousin to Yorkshire pudding eating contests,
And she listened, and encouraged, and advised, as she taught us,
And I'll miss her for sure when she's gone.

Oh who else was there my gullible son?,
Oh who else was there my darling young one?,
T'was someone called Linda, who had worked with the circus,
Enjoys tramping the fields, with a beagle called Barney,
Likes going to Eastbourne, with Emily and Charlotte,
Travels home and away, with hubbie and a camper-van,

And among other things, has been a turkey plucker.
She's a wife, she's a mother, a writer, and friend,
And I'll miss her for sure when this ends.

Oh who else was there my gullible son?,
Oh who else was there my darling young one?,
T'was someone called Kerry, who knits teapot covers,
And novelty items, and coats for her loved ones,
Who are two little dogs, called Dobbin and Muffin,
She keeps an allotment, and grows mini pumpkins,
And stands guard overnight, protecting the rhubarb,
And she writes, and she knits, and she walks, and she grows,
And I'll miss her for sure when she goes.

Was there anyone else there my gullible son?,
Was there anyone else there my darling young one?,
T'was someone called Sue, who loved eating chocolate,
A mum to two boys, and a mad dog called Bertie,
Who listed her hobbies, as writing and chocolate,
And described herself, as an ardent chocoholic,
Who enlisted in the army, at the age of eighteen.
And she writes, does the garden, eats chocolate, likes art,
And I'll miss her for sure when she departs.

Was there anyone else there my gullible son?,
Was there anyone else there my darling young one?,
T'was someone called Margaret, who browses antique shops,
Who like to do gardening, when she has time,
Who is an Industrial Emergency Planning Officer,
Keeping us safe, from Major Industrial accidents,
Who says she does nothing unusual or surprising.
And she writes, does the garden, buys antiques, keeps us safe,
And I'll miss her for sure when she's gone.

Oh who else was there my gullible son?,
Oh who else was there my darling young one?,
Someone called Victoria, who was small in stature,
Who takes after her grandma, a little cockney sparrow,
Whose family and friends, say she's a bit crazy,
Who loves the theatre, and treads the boards often,
Who'll be appearing quite soon in Calendar Girls

And she writes, and she acts, talks too much, loves her life,
And I'll miss her for sure when she's gone.

Oh who else was there my gullible son?,
Oh who else was there my darling young one?,
Someone called Christine, who works as a Village Agent,
Who says she's sex queen, and a domestic goddess,
Who was a Cruft's judge, and a custodian of tradition,
Who writes under different pseudonyms,
based on previous employment,
Who is her real self, in the blink of the moment.
And she writes, and she judges, has a headache, is a child,
And I'll miss her for sure when she's gone.

Oh who else was there my gullible son?,
Oh who else was there my darling young one?
Someone called Marion, who sings Carol King songs,
Who loves gardening, and poppies,
and cornflowers, and bluebells,
Who sings in the choir, and feeds the birds in her garden,
Who introduced me to astrolemerias,
Who sits on a deckchair at midnight, watching the stars.
And she writes, and she sings, sows seeds, and stargazes
And I'll miss her for sure when she's gone.

Oh who else was there my gullible son?,
Oh who else was there my darling young one?,
Someone called Sheena, who is a singer/songwriter,
A horse riding teacher, and a tarot card reader,
A wife and a mother, and a sister of the Earth,
Who loves music and animals, and spirituality and nature,
Who loves books and reading, and writing all about it.
And she rides, and she reads, and she writes, she's a witch,
And I'll miss her for sure when she's gone.

Oh who else was there my gullible son?,
Oh who else was there my darling young one?,
Someone called Anna, who likes writing funny stuff,
A rugby team manager, with leg warmers, and a clipboard,
Who loves socialising, but hates her Ford Mondeo,
Who loves baking cakes, and making jewellery,

Who doesn't like spiders, or musical theatre,.
And she writes, and she bakes, has warm legs, makes cakes,
And I'll miss her for sure when she's gone.

Oh who else was there my gullible son?,
Oh who else was there my darling young one?,
Someone called Estella, who was a teacher of dancing,
An uncivil servant, and a servense in Val d'Isere,
A chauffeur in Germany, and a pottery maker,
Who is only here to keep her off the streets,
Who chose her own name, and says she's dead ordinary,.
And she writes, breathes in, breathes out, throws pots,
And I'll miss her for sure when she's gone.

Oh who else was there my gullible son?,
Oh who else was there my darling young one?,
Someone called Dennis, who is a window cleaner,
Who is very keen, on music and singing,
Who does karaoke at the White Horse in Mundon,
Who was blessed with good fortune by a faith healer,
Who told him he would always have enough work,.
And he writes, and he plays, climbs ladders, and sings,
And I'll miss him for sure when he's gone.

What else is there to tell my gullible son?,
About you and your friends my darling young one?,
Well, "Who is Like God?", is a question for all of them,
Perhaps derived from a martyr, of the French Revolution.
An obvious moniker, for the Roman goddess of victory,
An Old Testament heroine, whose name means "lily",
Or a girl from the emerald isle, named for Ciar's people,
A "pearl" the patron saint, of expectant mothers,
Someone is soft and tender, and Spanish for "beautiful",
An Anglicized form, of the Scottish name Sine (Jeanne),
Traditionally the mother of the Virgin Mary,
A legendary saint, tormented by her pagan father,
In 6th century Brittany, was "handsome" or "little rock",
A 3rd century missionary, now the patron saint of France,
Miss Havisham in Dickens, with a name meaning "star",
And our names, are all here, no more strangers, all friends,
Fare thee well to you all, it's the end.

Departures

***If you've ever seen the very ancient movie, "Brief Encounter", starring Celia Johnson and Trevor Howard, then you may or may not recognise some parallels here. Lots of atmosphere created by steam-trains, unrequited love, and tsunamis of doubt. This was recorded at Highfield Studios on the CD album "Dangerous Curves".***
***Also, I had the privilege of performing this song at the Cramphorn Theatre in Chelmsford on 31st January, 2018.***

19th/22nd February 2012

Platform 4 on the edge of the morning,
Slamming doors, whistle-blown warning,
Thunder roars, ground shakes, wheels squealing,
Fare thee well my love, so sad to know you're leaving.
Was it just wishful thinking you blew me a kiss?,
As the train whistled by in the steam, and the smoke,
And the crisp morning air shrouded in mists,
Of the memories we shared,  Were you there?,
Or just somewhere else, deep down in my imagination,
I miss you, I miss you, I miss you.

Did I see your thin smile flash by in the window?,
Tears rolling down my cheeks in a torrent of sorrow,
A trick of the light in the hot smoky shadows?,
Destination tomorrow, loud locomotive echoes.
Was it just wishful thinking you blew me a kiss?,
As the train whistled by in the steam, and the smoke,
And the crisp morning air shrouded in mists,
Of the memories we shared,  Were you there?,
Or just somewhere else, deep down in my imagination,
I miss you, I miss you, I miss you.

Did you take a last quick glance, for the hint of a slim chance?,
A soft whispered whimsy, a flicker of nuance,
Were you stealing a glimpse, a swift flight of fancy?,
Lamenting our last dance, eclipse of a romance.
Yes! It was just wishful thinking you blew me a kiss?,
As the train whistled by in the steam, and the smoke,

And the crisp morning air shrouded in mists,
Of the memories we shared, You weren't there,
But just hidden somewhere, deep in my imagination,
I miss you, I miss you, I miss you.

Stirring words

***Because the original words were written in 1980, the inspiration is obviously lost in the fog of past ages. However, the words were rejigged in 2002 (22 years later?), and the tune was found after another 10 years.***
***The song was recorded at Highfield Studios on the CD album" And the Band Played On" in 2015.***

Originally circa 1980,
Lyrics completed August 2002
Music composed 14th March, 2012

As memories cascade from me, nostalgia cries to be set free,
Forgotten dreams, and fantasies, return from my infinity,
The clock has ticked; long ages spent, so seldom inspiration sent,
To steal the poet's zeal again, let magic gems flow from the pen,
To tear the dusty sheets apart, with stirring words, stirring words,
Stirring words, straight from the hear,

So sad the passing bloom of youth, that held reality aloof,
For as we grow long in the tooth, sad eyes reveal distorted truth,
Experience, the saving grace, to take enthusiasm's place,
It is by choice and not by chance, from circumstances thoughts advance,
And so by chance and not by choice, words may arrive, may arrive,
Words may arrive to raise a voice,

If only I was young again, with yearning heart burning as then,
To set new milestones in my mind, adventures of a different kind,
Just lurking in the atmosphere, a spark to light a new idea,
By accident, not by design, sweet reminiscence fills my time,
But by design, not accident. my time is lost, time is lost,
My time is lost as time is spent.

Dangerous Curves

***"I read a very interesting book called "Dangerous Curves" It was a documentary about oil exploration and the future energy requirements of a world based on fossil fuels. I liked the title and decided to use it to loosely document the time when I had been tailgated along the Baddow Bypass by a young man driving a Porsche.***
***Three verses came together, which show the need for speed, the promiscuous lifestyle, and the potential consequences of a too fast to live, too young to die attitude."***
***The song was recorded at Highfield Studios in June 2015 on the CD album Dangerous Curves".***

5th-10th April, 2012

I'm driving in my Porsche in the dead of night,
Roaring through the countryside, blazing headlights,
Pedal to the metal, squealing tyres and burning rubber,
Shifting through my gears beyond a hundred miles an hour,
I'm your tail-gaiter and I'm bringing up your rear,
I don't want no motorways, no straight roads, or low gears,
Want to feel the G-force, the horsepower, and the swerve,
Man I'm just a petrol-head on dangerous curves,
Dangerous curves, dangerous curves,
Man I'm just a petrol-head on dangerous curves,
Running my wheels over dangerous curves,
Showing my skills on dangerous curves,
Moving in for the kill on dangerous curves.
Man I'm just a petrol-head on dangerous curves.

Dressed up in my finery for nightlife on the pull,
Wallet stuffed with ready cash, attitude full of bull (shit),
Not looking for that special someone, no just a one night stand,
No long term commitment babes, no-one ties my hands,
I'm God's gift to women, you know I'm the man,
Got the looks, got the dosh, ain't no also-ran,
No computer dating, can't get what I deserve,
Looking for a lady with dangerous curves,
Dangerous curves, dangerous curves,

Looking for a lady with dangerous curves,
Kissing and caressing those dangerous curves,
Counting my blessings for dangerous curves,
Ain't doing no confessing on dangerous curves.
Looking for a lady with dangerous curves.

I went to see the doctor; I was feeling below par,
Drove there at breakneck speed in my turbo charged car,
He fixed monitor wires to my body and my head,
He umm'd and ah'd, and took some notes, and this is what he said,
I've been looking at your test results, so let's not pretend,
Someone here's been burning the candle at both ends,
You'd better slow down my friend, you been living on your nerves,
There's overwhelming evidence for dangerous curves,
Dangerous curves, dangerous curves,
There's overwhelming evidence for dangerous curves,
Live fast, die young, on dangerous curves,
Won't last too long on dangerous curves,
One day you'll die on dangerous curves.
There's overwhelming evidence for dangerous curves.

## Pretty Red Dress

***When Gerry Rafferty died on 4th January, 2011, I wanted to write something relative to Baker Street, and this was the first offering.***

Written 21st Jan, to 2nd Feb 2011, revised 17th April, 2012

Somewhere deep in the gloom, of those strange catacombs,
A raven-haired lass, in a pretty red dress,
And the swirl and the swoon, of that Rafferty tune,
Swoops and circles around, in the caverns underground.
She's a long way from home, playing wild saxophone,
Close to where we meet, at Baker Street.

The super sleuths look, through the clues in the good book,
They're chilling out on cocaine, as she's waiting for another train,
And she begins once again, when the next train pulls in,
The grandfather clock chimes, while they dwell on the crimes,
She's a long way from home, playing wild saxophone,
Close to 221b Baker Street.

Where wise men can converse, the mysteries of the Universe,
So stargazers pretend, they understand, and comprehend,
It's so cleverly explained, But there's still a nagging pain,
In this over-crowded place, we can all get lost in space.
Is it all just a dream when no one hears you scream?
Close to where we meet, at Baker Street.

This city is guilty of selling illusion,
Fiction and fantasy, both fuelling confusion,
Just yesterday's heroes, and celebrity zeroes,
All our tomorrows, in the chamber of horrors.
And in her man-made black hole, she moves body and soul,
She's light years from home playing wild saxophone,

If this city is a desert, and devoid of any soul,
But we have to face the facts, there ain't nowhere else to go,
But after the man and the mystery have gone,
The music,
Goes on.

## A Kiss Goodnight

***We were set a homework exercise to write a highly structured form of poem called a villanelle. This is one of the results, which can be translated very easily to a song format.***

19th April, 2012

A kiss goodnight is all I ask,
To soothe me to my sleep, If that is not too hard a task.

A tipple from your loving flask,
To savour and to keep, A kiss goodnight is all I ask.

And then within your smile I bask,
As through the night I creep, If that is not too hard a task.

Before I slip behind night's mask,
And pretend to be Bo-peep, A kiss goodnight is all I ask.

And hoping that the moment lasts,
I go off counting sheep, If that is not too hard a task.

When my slumbers have come to pass,
And I awake from the deep,
A kiss goodnight was all I asked,
If that was not too hard a task.

Drought

***Here's another even better villanelle. Do you think so?***

19th April, 2012

Sometimes the rain stays in the sky,
Parched land is dry and bare,
When thunder clouds go rolling by.

And rain gods hide aloof and shy,
Hoarding their precious wares,
Sometimes the rain stays in the sky.

The weatherman will wonder why,
We wander in despair,
When thunder clouds go rolling by.

To quench Earth's thirst and satisfy,
Our poor land's pleading prayer,
Sometimes the rain stays in the sky.

Our barren brook meanders dry,
If rainy days are spared,
When thunder clouds go rolling by.

We cannot let the flowers die,
When rainfall is so rare,
Sometimes the rain stays in the sky,
When thunder clouds go rolling by.

"Punk Piece" Another turn of the screw

***The homework exercise this time was to write a story or poem entitled "A Punk Piece".***
***The result was this unstructured poem.***

5th/7th August, 2012

I pour scorn on this world where I wasn't born,
Floating in a swamp of mediocrity, pretending to be reality,
An ocean of war and hypocrisy,
masquerading as peace and democracy.
Politicians come and go, and tell us what to say and do,
They line their pockets with our dough,
and disappear into their altruistic blue.
Communism didn't work because of people's greed,
But capitalism only works to fill the greedy need.
Benefits cut, shops and factories shut, you and me get the chop,
Workers laid off, bosses profits up as they cream it off the top,
Bankers caused the slump, and now they take a dump,
Shitting on the rest of us, still racking up their bonuses.
And all the time they eat away at our freedoms,
Like some insidious little squirming worm,
Slowly, slowly turns the screw,
To every season turn, turn, turn.

What can I say, what can I do, to not offend or undermine?
Political correctness rules the day, to tell the truth may be a
crime, It used to be that you could tell a joke, or have a poke,
at anyone just for fun, Now you can't call something what it is,
in case you offend someone.
Once there were queers, now they're called gay,
And they no longer get locked away,
They're all coming out, not staying in,
And what they get up to is no more a sin,
And I'm a homophobic because of what I say,
Even though I have no irrational fear of the games they play.
It's now racist to call someone black,
And Irish jokes are a xenophobic attack,
It's the thin end of the wedge, the edge of a ledge, a precipice,
We're about to fall into, a cunning, clever, contrived abyss.

So how long will it be before to say it's raining cats and dogs,
Will be deemed offensive by animal lovers?
Too many cooks spoil the broth, an insult to chefs or Heinz soups?
Give a dog a bad name, to get up the noses of all dogs,
Or just dogs with good names like Rex or Rover?

And now the world of the young is hung with pneumatic,
neurotic women, and pathetic, despotic men,
So the con-trick prevails and we all just fail,
On the same old merry-go-round again.
And they're still eating away at our freedoms,
That insidious little worm still squirming,
To every season turn, turn, turn,
Slowly, slowly the inscrutable screw is turning.

I'm persuaded to say nothing, to do much more than less,
Just wallow in apathetic, and revel in the mess,
Swim in the cesspit, climb on the shit heap,
swallow all the crap,
And keep it buttoned, lips sealed, eyes closed,
ears plugged, comatose.

Ghost of a Ploughman
or Fair Poppy Fields of France

***I think the subject for the Maldon Writing Group homework was" Ghost", and for some reason I thought back to the First World War and a poem I had written in 1998 called "Armistice". This is where I revisit the battlefields of the war to end all wars with a slightly different slant.***
***Perhaps it's a more brash and cynical view, and it's certainly not a simplistic and faint hearted one.***
***Perhaps I have mellowed in the intervening 14 years?***

12th September, 2012

When jingoism swayed me to patriotic fervour,
And posters so ubiquitous drove enthusiasm further,
Kitchener's pointing finger declared
the Empire surely needs me,
I signed up quick, and agreed to go
where King and Country lead me,
To be on the side of victory and justice for my God,
Not an unknown soldier in a lonely cemetery,
a piece of cannon fodder.

Then the noises of battle flooded my ears,
Like an avalanche in my head,
And surrounded me with blood-curdling screams,
From the dying and the dead,
And the air was so foul, like breathing soup,
Bursting my lungs like the devil's embrace,
While the ripping hail sought to impale me,
Like shards of glass on my face.

Then every trench had the stench of death,
From battered, bitter corpses,
While every man fought for every breath,
Among dismembered, bloated horses,
I was tramping in my trench foot boots,
In the mud, and the blood, and skinny starving rats,
There was only one exit from this hell,
And it's not shown on the general's maps.

When the last whistle blew we flew over the top,
Brothers in arms, and yet we all know,
Kitchener's a lying, warmongering bastard,
Now why did we say we would go?,
Oh Yes!, We were persuaded to join up,
When they led all our boys a merry old dance,
And all we are now are the ghosts of a ploughman,
In the fair poppy fields of France.

The Dignity of the Moment (No Easy Way)

***I think this is yet another example of me mourning a love lost, but in a different more positive (?) way.***

6th November, 2012

There's a tell-tale echo in the look upon your face,
Suggests you've been telling me lies,
A question in the way that you fix your gaze on me,
Arrests the reflections in your eyes,
Now there's a great hollow space in the heart of my heart,
But you tell me there is no other way,
It's down to you move on, and me to be abandoned,
And it seems there's nothing more for us to say,
Can I sacrifice my feelings to the dignity of the moment,
And just walk slowly away?

Please don't hurt me again,
Please don't make me cry,
We both know there is no easy way,
No easy way to say goodbye.

It comes as no surprise that we're in this situation,
Something has been brooding for some time,
That emptiness between us that's been growing unabated,
While our closeness has been withering on the vine,
We slowly slid to this impasse as the world went on around us,
Though there can be no rhyme nor reason to defend,
The moving finger writes and having writ moves on,
And everything must die we cannot mend,
I'll keep a reign on my emotions,
grasp some dignity in the moment,
And accept that this is the end.

You won't hurt me again,
You won't make me cry,
We both know there is no easy way,
No easy way to say goodbye.

## Angel's Holiday

***Where the inspiration for this story of a "holiday" with a difference came from, I am not sure. There are obviously some references to song lyrics in the story, and if you were to ask me if I've actually visited the "holiday destination", and suffered the atmosphere that hangs over that place, then the answer is "Yes, I have, and I don't wish to repeat the experience. This story eventually became a chapter in my novel "Angel's Rainbow". There is a lesson in this tale that all aspiring angels, good or bad, need to learn from."***

3rd December, 2012

It's been a very long, time that I've been training to be an angel, and I have to say that I have enjoyed every minute of it. I remember I started with simple things like sewing crystals made from raindrops on the edges of clouds so that they would all have a silver lining. I spent some time knitting sunbeams together in the right order to make rainbows, and making sure that they were positioned not to touch the ground, so that another angel didn't need to hide a pot of gold at each end. I loved all the nights I spent catching falling stars, and putting them in my pocket, and saving them for a rainy day. I became so good at it Gabriel gave me a special purple pouch to put my falling stars in, so that they would never fade away. They were very special because when I needed them I could use them to perform magical deeds. When I wasn't doing these things I would often be found sitting on a favourite cloud playing on my very own harp, and winding harp strings from angel hair.
Guardian angel duty was always very rewarding. All angels got special assignments looking after someone who needed a bit of help. It was especially wonderful sitting over someone's shoulder, and whispering to them to save them from harm or danger. Sometimes, it was just a matter of creating a timely distraction, like a sudden burst of sunlight through the clouds, or a breath of a cool calming breeze on a very hot day. Maybe a snowflake landing on an eyelash, or a bird suddenly starting to sing in a tree. Anything that was a nice surprise, just to stop them for a moment until the danger had passed. I loved this kind of angel work.

At the end of one day, as I was just idly swinging on a star, I was asked to go and see Gabriel. He told me that he was so pleased with my progress that I had been assigned a holiday.
"What is a holiday?" I asked Gabriel, "And what will I be doing?"
He just said I'd have to wait and see, because holidays were always great mysteries, were randomly allocated, and he couldn't tell me where I would be going, just that it would be very soon. I went back to my duties.
I was carrying some moonbeams home in a jar, wondering what my holiday would be, when I bumped into my old friend Sebastian and he told me what an honour it was if you were assigned a holiday. He advised me that it gave you a chance to do something nasty, wicked or evil, but you had to very, very careful because there were always consequences.
I pressured him into telling me about his last holiday, and after a great deal of persuasion, he swore me to absolute secrecy. Then he said that on his last holiday which had been three aeons and a day ago, he had been sent to Jerusalem, and he had been a Roman soldier on crucifixion duty. The job he was assigned to do was to hammer in one of the nails that put Jesus on the cross. But he wouldn't go into any more detail about what happened. He just said "You'll be fine my friend, if you do the right thing!"
When I tried to sleep that night I was nervous and excited, and I kept waking up with a strange word resounding in my head. It started as a whisper, and then each time I woke up it got louder and louder and louder.
"Oswiecim"
"Oswiecim"
"OSwiecim"
"OSWIECIM!"
The next morning when I woke up, I wasn't on my beautiful cloud with a silver lining, sewn by my own fair hand. I was in a very different place. It was a crude wooden hut, and I was wearing a smart black uniform. It was very cold; snow had fallen overnight but was covered by a layer of grey ash. There was an awful burnt, charred, sickly smell. I was very afraid.
Suddenly there was a lot of commotion and shouting outside, and the clanking, squealing, rushing steam noise of a train arriving, and I heard strange words like "Raus! Raus!" and "Schnell! Schnell!" ringing in my ears. The door of my hut burst open, with a rush of icy chill which cut right through me, and then

someone came in to get me. He had a stern, grim face and he ushered me out into the cold, and told me where to stand.
Lots of very sad bedraggled people piled off the train, and were quickly led up to a very important looking man at a desk. He waved any man who looked big and strong to his right. And all the puny, or disabled, or weak old men, together with all the women and children, even women with babies, were herded to his left. Any belongings or suitcases they had brought with them were quickly stacked up and then taken away. Anyone who made any fuss or protest was frogmarched behind a nearby wall, and behind that wall I heard screams and shouts and gunshots.
Snow and ash were both still falling, and it was bitterly cold. The wind howled cruelly between the buildings in the darkness of a gruesome early morning. There were no smiles, no affection, and no compassion in this terrible place. The left hand queue were led away and ordered to strip off, and when they asked why, they were told with cynical sneering looks, that they were going to be showered and deloused. Eventually they were led down some steps into a big very bare room with water pipes sticking out of the ceiling. Once everybody had been herded inside two sets of heavy double iron doors were closed and a straight iron bar placed across them.
"You! You're new aren't you?" said Mr Important, looking at me
"Yes sir" I responded scared out of my wits.
"You can do the dirty deed then." he instructed.
He snarled each instruction in short sentences and phrases.
"Climb up that ladder to the top of the roof. Up there you'll find a pair of heavy gloves and a mask. Be careful to put them on. Then take one of the cans from the top of the roof. Twist the top, turn it upside down, and drop it through the hole. Leave the gloves and mask up there. Hold your breath. Climb down as quickly as you can."
I did as I was told terrified, to shouts of "Schnell! Schnell!"
Just as I was going to drop the can, Mr Important shouted "Halt!" and everybody ducked.
There was a very loud rumbling noise coming from the East as a stricken plane coughed and spluttered over, flying very low, with thick black smoke belching out of its engine. Everybody looked up and felt sorry for the poor pilot trapped inside, and then it crashed in a ball of flame, and an awful ground shaking explosion a few fields away.

Moments later Mr Important nodded at me and I carried on as instructed.
"Let's go for breakfast, and come back when it's over" suggested one of the black uniforms, "I don't want to listen to THAT again and again." We all shivered our way into another large wooden hut. There was a small wood burning stove in the corner, some bare wooden tables and stools, and at least it was some respite from the all-pervading stench of burning, and the unrelenting bitterness of the wind. There was a calendar on the otherwise bare wall, and I sneaked a look at the date. It was December 24th 1943. The calendar didn't have a picture of a lovely landscape, or seascape, or flowers, or happy smiling faces, just a very stern looking man with a peculiar moustache and pure evil in his eyes. We ate quietly, each man a small piece of sausage, a lump of stale bread, and some ersatz coffee.
"A Messerschmitt me109 wasn't it?" questioned one of the black uniforms," Coming back from the Russian front."
Nobody answered. "Poor bastards!" he continued.
Breakfast was over soon enough. "Now the gruesome work begins." muttered another black uniform, as we all moved back out into the cold. He moved the big iron bar, and opened the first set of double iron doors. There was a strange translucent green light just visible through the small cracks in the second set of iron doors. With a great heavy clang he threw them open, and took a deep breath, before stepping down into what was now an every day, several times a day, sight. But instead of the expected pile of contorted bodies, with tortured screaming faces, and the stench of prussic acid and shit, he found the room was empty. As he focussed his eyes in utter disbelief, and hesitated on the second step down, the green light seemed to swirl like a ghostly whirlpool. Then a stream of a million blindingly bright twinkling stars, curved in a magnificent continuous light show, making their way in a glorious triumphant free ribbon up into the blackness of the heavens.
"What's going on?" roared Mr Important.
"I don't know," answered the black uniform in the doorway, "But the room is empty."
"That's impossible!" hurled a now very angry voice.
"Come and look for yourself." was my reply.
All the other black uniformed men stared into the room, and for a short while stood there baffled. What none of them knew, was

that when they were all distracted by the plane's swansong overhead, I had quietly and quickly put the can back on the roof, and re-tightened the top. Then without anyone noticing I took my purple pouch out of my pocket, and dropped that into the hole in the roof instead.

The black uniforms all gathered around Mr Important, and they started shouting and pointing at me. I stood there shivering in the cold, and then they ran over to me still shouting and dragged me away. They tied my hands behind my back and placed me up against a wall. Weapons were primed as they assembled for a firing squad, but even then for some reason all my fear had left me.

I prayed quietly to myself, closed my eyes, and waited for the bullets to rip into me. But as I felt each one go into my heart I found it didn't hurt. No! Not at all!

Each bullet felt like someone was kissing me very gently, and when the last bullet hit me right between the eyes, then the whole universe swirled round and round for what seemed like ages.

When I opened my eyes I was back on my favourite cloud, and Sebastian was sitting next to me. "How was your holiday?" he asked smiling.

"Er, OK" I replied, obviously looking a bit confused.

"You did the right thing, my friend." he smiled again," Or you wouldn't be back here now"

And with that we carried on catching falling stars and putting them in our pockets, and saving them for a rainy day.

# CHAPTER 4

## A Few Days in the Life of a Man with a Porsche

***"He reminded Norman as often as he could***
***that Evian spelt backwards was "naive",***
***and claimed that only boys drank Lucozade lookalikes,***
***real men drank real beer; Guinness, bitter,***
***and certainly not that pisswater they called lager."***

A few days in the life of a man with a Porsche.

***After writing the song "Dangerous Curves", and performing it at the writer's group, the suggested homework was to write a story based upon the personality of the Porsche driver. I invented someone called Norman Noble, and he came to life in "A Few Days in the Life of a Man with a Porsche"***
***Eventually in a different form the story became the first chapter of my publishing debut novel, "Chelmsford 2012 - Many Hearts One Mind".***

14th June, 2012

Friday 8 am:
The clock radio alarm burst into life, and the well heard voices of Heart FM and Martin and Sue introduced another play of "Tonight's gonna be a good, good night".
Norman Noble opened one eye and looked very briefly at the red digits on the face of the alarm. Hmm! 7.59. Then he realised there was someone lying next to him
in the bed, and propped up on one arm dared to take a peep. His eyes panned slowly from the ample bosom heaving suggestively under the thin duvet, to a
mass of dyed blonde hair, smudged make up, still asleep, but only just, awful red lipstick, reminding him of his mum. He rubbed the sleep from his eyes, and focussed a little more bravely. Grey hair at the temples, 3 chins, wrinkly neck, "Oh my God!" he whispered" It's whatshername, erm, Caroline, from the Two Brewers, "Shit! I've been cougared, "Oh, how will I live this down?"
Caroline stirred and blinked awake, and looked at Norman. He smiled a thin nervous smile, struggled for something to say, and quietly slurred, "HI sweetie, how was it for you?"
"Only 6 hours too late for it to matter at all" thought Caroline, but answered convincingly " Wonderful"
"Good" he replied, and quickly turned, sat on the side of the bed, and got up, ready to go for a quick shower.
"Hung like a horse, that's me" he thought,
"Yeah! A sea horse" thought Caroline.
"I've got to go off to work", offered Norman " Why don't you have

a little doze, I'll bring you a coffee, and then you can leave when you're ready, Let yourself out"
"OK", she replied snuggling back into the bed, thinking "How sweet", not realising that all Norman was doing was making sure they didn't leave his apartment in
The Hub together, and have any of his neighbours bump into them, and see him and Desperate Caroline in close proximity.

8.45 am
The Porsche Carrera 911 engine roared, and Norman slid out onto Springfield Road, making for the A12 and Colchester.
Gunned it on the slip-road at the Cramphorn flyover, looked at his watch, and gave it the turbo large.
"18 minutes, to the office, easy".
He popped out a Coldplay CD, and pushed it into the player.
"Para, para, paradise", sang Chris Martin, and Norman joined in as best he could.
"Barret, barret, barret eyes", he wasn't at his best due the busted lip Caroline had inflicted on him just before he left.
Perhaps, he shouldn't have asked her "Can you make sure you leave quietly?"

9:10 am
The office of NERDSOFT sprang into view, Norman smiled,
"Right on time, Yeah!"
He leaned over and opened his leather briefcase, retrieved some papers, and gave himself a congratulatory splash of Erection aftershave,
"Now! who's at the meeting? It was the usual crew:
Company Chairman Tim (Tiny) Gonads, his boss, smart, good suit, silk tie, patent leather shoes.
Hugh Jarse was the incredibly obese Marketing Director, scruffy, old cheap suit, no tie, brown shoes.
Gordon Bullock (affectionately known as Golden Bollocks) the Company Accountant, dapper, silver grey hair, 3 piece pin-striped suit, Gucci shoes
and of course himself, listed as a boardroom in-joke Norman Nobless, Development Director. best dressed bloke by far, modern man about town.
He was proud of his position, and the way he had acquired it.
Not academically bright, Norman had spent all his teenage years

,and a few of his twenties, studying the only thing he had ever been good at. He was a self-confessed computer games super nerd, had dissected every game and sussed out the way to write the software for all of them.

He knew every line of the programs for Super Mario, Sonic the Hedgehog, Modern Warfare 1, 2 and 3, Grand Theft Auto, Assassins, all of them. He had reached top level on every game he'd ever played, bar none.
At 23 he had written a game called Viking Ninja Holocaust 9, perfected it, meticulously prepared the artwork etc. and marched up to Tiny at the Computerworld Exhibition in Earls Court and challenged him to beat him at the game. Tiny's computer games skill was legendary, and he had never been beaten, but after 30 minutes of VNH9 (as Norman called it) he was hooked and baffled, and offered Norman a job at NERDSOFT on the spot.
Now the success of the company hung on Norman's fevered brain, and his next computer game, like a spider on a damp autumn morning web.
The lads had all grown fat and lazy on it, especially Hugh. But Norman had looked after himself, sure he was top nerd, but he was well-groomed, fairly slim, not unfit, and liked to think of himself as someone waiting for a call (any day now!) from the production team of the next series of The Only Way is Essex. He idolised Mark Bright. He loved every series of Big Brother. And, he hid his Yorkshire upbringing and particularly his accent under a veil of acquired Essex boy speak.

9:15 am
Norman grabbed himself a Frappuccino, and sat down next to Tim. The boys were already deep in frantic argument about who was best at the karaoke last night at the Two Brewers, and Norman wondered why the board meetings were always on a Friday at the NERDSOFT Offices in Colchester when all of them now lived in Chelmsford. Tiny had only recently moved there from East Bergholt, which is how he came up with the company name of North Essex Research and Development Software after he had written a mildly successful Word Processing program. Norman shuffled in his seat and coughed nervously not to draw too much attention, and hoped that none of them had seen him leave with desperate Caroline.

He hadn't been drunk and incapable, so it wasn't a loss of memory problem, and nowadays he only drank Evian water, and Isotonic sports drinks.
The lads ribbed him about it, especially Hugh who saw bottled water as a huge marketing con, and only drank draft Guinness. He reminded Norman as often as he could that Evian spelt backwards was "naive", and claimed that only boys drank Lucozade lookalikes, real men drank real beer; Guinness, bitter, and certainly not that pisswater they called lager.
Norman had only been drunk once is life, because after his 18th birthday party he had woken up the next morning stark bollock naked and shackled by hand and foot
to the top of a bus shelter in Danbury. He couldn't remember a single thing about how he got there till this day, and had vowed never to get in that state again.

9:31 am
"Christ, Norman! What have you done" asked Tiny, "Did you trip over your wallet?".
"No!" He smirked, and thought he'd test the water " Remember when we left the Brewers last night? he paused.
"Can't remember a thing, far too pissed to care" they all grinned at each other and answered in unison.
"Good" thought a relieved Norman, and then added" Some brainless oik was puking up on my Porsche, so I picked him up and gave him a right pasting"
" He got a lucky slap on me once, cut my lip, but now he's probably in intensive care, having breakfast through a straw". Nobody believed him , but all agreed, "Nice one Norm".

The meeting droned on as usual, taking the standard route; Tiny gave his best "We're a big company, in a little office, running on a shoestring, must grow and prosper" speech. Hugh puffed his way through a rain forest of reports outlining the same marketing strategy he'd trumpeted for a least 5 years. Good old Golden Bollocks produced graphs, pie charts and spreadsheets showing the company was still making a healthy profit, and discussed projections for the next financial year.

Norman, was always last, but he knew he was keeping the company going with his ideas. He presented early versions of 2

new games he was working on.
Everybody loved R McGeddon's Nerd World Apocalypse, and it was gone 3 pm before they'd all finished playing Beer Festival Bastards Final Frontier.

3:30 pm
Norman left and drove back through the country lanes, listening to Coldplay again, whistling through Stanway, Tiptree, Maldon, and Hatfield Peveril, before smashing through the gears onto the last bit of the A12. Soon he was back in his pad in The Hub. Thankfully Desperate Caroline had gone, but not before she'd trashed the bathroom, smudged "Arseholes" in very red lipstick on all the wardrobes, and thrown all 15 pairs of his Calvin Klein boxer shorts over the balcony into the River Chelmer.
He could see them floating in a line in the reeds, all the way up to Tescos. "I'll collect them up later, when it's dark" he thought.

3:45 pm
The phone rang, "Ey Oop! Son" the familiar voice of Stanley, Norman's dad " 'Ow yer diddlin'".
"Alright Dad, How are you?
"Mustn't grumble, nobody listens anyway".
"Mum alright, is she?"
"Aye son, same as ever"
"What can I do for you Dad?"
"Well, I'm just phoning up to remind thee 'bout t' game tomorrow. You know t' 'ockey match yer sister's playing in,
Oh, and yer Mum says stay for lunch after, and she'll do yer fav'rit"
"OK Dad, I hadn't forgotten, I'll be there about 10, see you then, love to Mum."
"Bye son, drive carefully".

"Oh, horror of horrors," thought Norman, "not again.".
Every couple of weeks his sister, the unfortunately named Cher, yes Cher Noble, played hockey for a local team. Cher was built like her mother, like Geoff Capes on steroids; in fact she looked a bit like Geoff Capes without the beard. Her hockey team were called the Norfolk Enchants, they always lost, it was always a family affair, and Norman always hated it, but felt obliged to go

along.
Sometimes all the families stood there in the freezing cold, trying to drum up some enthusiasm, chanting away, and it sounded really encouraging in Stanley's Yorkshire accent " Norfolk Enchants,  Norfolk Enchants" , Cher would play her socks off to no avail, come off with badly bruised legs, covered in mud and cow-pats in various states of fermentation, and give Norman a big sisterly hug. "Yuk!" It was dire, and it got worse.

Saturday 12:15 pm
Cher as always insisted on coming back to the bungalow near Leiston, on the accurately named New Clear View estate, covered in excrement. Norman fretted about yet another expensive valet for the Porsche, and how quickly he could get rid of the stink. Stanley and Lisalotte returned in their clapped out Mondeo.

He loved his Mum and Dad, but they were the oddest couple on the planet, Stanley, in his heavy tweed suit, thick set, bushy moustache, yellow, fag-stained teeth, unmistakable Yorkshire clichés, and Lisalotte, of German stock, posh frock, too much very red lipstick, pigeon English at best.
They had met at the Munich Beer Festival, when Stanley and a group of master butchers, for that was his trade, had gone on his once in a lifetime trip abroad.
Lisalotte was one of those strappingly built serving wenches, a great bustling clod-hopper of a girl, who could carry 8 huge steins of beer without spilling a drop.
Having never been abroad before, Stanley mistook her beery bonhomie for some kind of mutual attraction, and had invited her to a bockwurst eating contest. Surprisingly she had obliged, only to eat him under the table. Sausages were his life's work, and he was gutted when she beat him.

But it was the start of a beautiful relationship, and within a month she had moved to Yorkshire, and they had married by special license. Sausages was all they had in common!
Life was kind to both of them, and Stanley's butchery business thrived, until that irrepressible berk Chester Gannet came on the scene, and screwed it up for them, forcing them to sell up, and retire to Suffolk.

The story goes that every year in mid-June Stanley made a fortune after perfecting what he called Stanley's Seasonal Burgundian, a sausage with an unusual, but very popular twang. He guarded a secret recipe, created a sausage with true rarity value, and managed to sell them to some very posh shops and restaurants.
Even the Queen ordered them from Fortnum and Mason's.
Nobody knew the real secret of his success.
But several years ago, they had built a new bypass around the village of Kirby Wiske, and this forced the local frog population to find a new migration route to the River Swale at the back of his butcher's premises. Stanley came home one night quite late from the local pub, The Cricketers, and ran over and squashed thousands of migrating frogs on the road outside. Never one to miss an opportunity he wheelbarrowed them all into his shop, and invented a recipe to use them in an exotic foreign sausage. But the migration took place always for 10 nights on the trot, so eventually he had absolutely thousands and thousands of squashed frogs to turn into sausages.
It was a windfall, oh and a frog squash.
He reasoned that the French ate frogs legs, and what was the harm in using the whole frog, beautifully tenderised by the tyres of his butcher's van, and then made fresh into the finest sausages he could imagine.
And then after 5 successful years, and fame and some small fortune, bloody Chester Gannet sent a spy out to the village, and accidentally found out what Stanley was doing, and exposed the scandal of the Seasonal Burgundian. Him of all people, with his pretentious crap infested concoctions. He was just jealous.
The scandal broke when Lisalotte, never the brightest button in the box, was being interviewed on Yorkshire TV News, and innocently referred to Stanley's Seasonal Burgundian as a " zoze Froggy Bangers". Suspicions were raised, Chester Gannet protested, and pretty soon it got to the front page of the Northallerton Echo.
Anyway, that was the end, Lisalotte had a nervous breakdown, and shortly after they had to sell up, and move, and become anonymous.

Saturday 1 pm
Norman screeched to a halt outside the bungalow, he persuaded Cher to get out and have bath, the smell of sweat and cow-pat was overpowering, and 10 minutes later Stanley and Lisalotte arrived in the Mondeo.
"Come in sohn," said Lisalotte,"take your shoes off, and pur uz all a drink, zere's some Blue Nun for ous, an Adam's beer for you Dad (she never could say Adnam's), Oh, and of course some Perry wasser for you my dearest boy." She always gets it wrong" thought Norman.
Polite chit-chat followed, and soon the bockwurst and sauerkraut were ready. Norman hated bockwurst, loathed sauerkraut, but scoffed enthusiastically to please his Mum.

Later, Stanley and Norman made for the garden so Dad could show off his roses and his prize rhubarb. By this time Mum and sister had quaffed 3 bottles of Blue Nun between them, and were both snoring contentedly legs akimbo on the sofa. Dad loved his garden, and Norman appeased him by showing a bit of interest.
"Come and 'ave a butcher's at this" said Stanley, strolling towards his greenhouse.
"I'm growing this funny plant for Sid up t' road, you know, 'im what lives in t' flats, 'e sez it's 'erbal; helps him with his arthritis".
They entered the greenhouse, damp and humid, and filled floor to ceiling with a prolific green mass of foliage. Norman didn't have the heart to tell his Dad what it was.
" Sid dried these leaves and made us some cakes with this once, Ah tell thee lad, they didn't taste of booze, but I think he laced them with it"
" Me and yer Mum, both felt like we'd had 10 pints down t' Cricketers, it took me 3 days to get back to feeling right again"
Norman grinned, and longed for the open road, Coldplay, and a turbo fix.
Soon after Norman, said his goodbyes and jumped into the Porsche, breathed a big sigh of relief, and burnt some rubber.
" 62 minutes dead on" he chuckled, as he pulled into his parking space back at the Hub in Chelmsford.

Saturday 8pm
Showered, shaved, preened, moisturised Norman was ready. All except he had to go commando due to a sudden shortage of

boxer shorts. Never mind, another generous splash of Erection aftershave, and Norman was on his way, down to Brentwood, to Sugar Hut, to try and be spotted by the scouts for The Only Way is Essex.

Sunday 8 am
The clock radio alarm burst into life, and the well heard voices of Heart FM and somebody other than Martin and Sue introduced another play of "Tonight's gonna be a good, good night". Norman Noble opened one eye and looked very briefly at the red digits on the face of the alarm. Hmm! 7.59. Then he realised there was someone lying next to him in the bed, and propped up on one arm dared to take a peep. His eyes panned slowly from the fine bronzed leg sticking out the side of the thin duvet, to a mass of dyed red hair, perfect make up, still asleep, but only just, understated light pink lipstick. He rubbed the sleep from his eyes, and focussed, with a wry smile, a little more keenly.
"Blimey! Not bad" he thought, " must have been a lucky night"
"Hang on, think quick, what is her name? Got it, Clarissa, Phew!"
Clarissa stirred and blinked awake, and looked at Norman. He smiled a big toothy smile, and quietly whispered "HI sweetie, how was it for you?"
"It's a bit late to ask now" thought Clarissa, but answered convincingly "You were wonderful, big boy"
"Good" he replied, and quickly turned full towards her, kissed her on the mouth, forgetting all about his busted lip, and enfolded her in his arms.
"How about a quick replay then?".
"Oooooohhh! Yeeees!" enthused Clarissa.

Sunday 8:30 am
"I've finished in the bathroom now" grinned Clarissa, " Sorry, but I've got to nip back home, and then get to St Mary's by 9:30, I'm singing in the choir this morning, will I see you again?"
Norman got up, grinned at Clarissa and jumped into the shower, " I do hope so"
The luscious feel of the warm water was running all over him from head to foot as Clarissa opened the shower door, gave him a quick peck on the lips,
followed by an affectionate tug on his willy, smiled, turned and went.

Norman didn't quite catch what she said as she left due to the noise of the running water in his ears, but it sounded like " I must tell you (pause) I've got to see Phyliss".
"Never mind, whatever it was it can wait" he mused, contented.

Monday 10:30 am
Norman was in the gents urinals trying to squeeze in alongside Hugh.
"Where were you Saturday Nobless, we missed you down the Brewers, no one to take the piss out of?"
"Oh I went to Sugar Hut, picked up this lovely bit of stuff, Clarissa's her name.".
Hugh laughed, " Good looking bird, red hair, nice make up, sings in the church choir".
"Yeah, that's her, do you know her?
"Yes mate, and there's something you should know.".
"What's that?"
Hugh stepped back from the urinal, didn't wash his hands, and before he turned and left the room, he raised his hands above his head, and clapped just once, and let out a strange cry like he was a fat demented seal at a marine park. Norman looked down still peeing himself, now in panic, " Oh My God!"

# CHAPTER 5

## Something Other than the Colours

***"But every time I tried,***
***My thoughts were cast aside,***
***By an another idea that was languishing on the shelf."***

Upside Down

***The subject was simply "Upside Down". There may have about quangos on the TV news at the time that sparkedthe inspiration. In the times of recession where David Cameron said "We are all in it together." it was a bit obvious that the quango committee members are not in it with us, and neither are the bonus munching bankers (rhymes with something that they could be called),who got us into the financial mess in the first place. The Prime Minister's statement perhaps should be amended to "You are all in the (sh)it together.***

4th January, 2013

*Imagine that you are at a major conference centre in London. It is 11:30 am, on 22nd December, 2012, and the auditorium is full with men in well-cut suits, and power-dressed women. All of the assembled throng are bankers, stockbrokers, and financial sector bigwigs high on their generous bonuses, and looking forward to another free junket.*
*They are waiting to be addressed by the chairman of a government sponsored quango. A smartly dressed professorial type enters the stage, and the audience lulls quickly to silence.*

Allow me to introduce myself, and the reason why I am here having the privilege of talking to you today.
First of all my name is Professor Mac Sasiti, and my credentials are well known as a regular contributor to an extensive range of governmental research projects not only in Britain, but also throughout the European Economic Community.
I am so glad to have the opportunity to report to you today the universally important findings of our latest research project.
So, let me begin by telling you how this project came about, and then as I explain further, I am sure you will realise why it is so important to our future, our children's future, and our children's, children's future. To put no finer point upon it, what I shall shortly illustrate to you today, will fundamentally affect the continued development and survival of the human race.
Six months ago, I met with Deputy Prime Minister, Nick Clegg at 10, Downing Street as he was worried about the predictions of

the Mayan civilisation that the world would come to an end on 21st December, 2012. Various hypothesis were put forward as to how the end would manifest itself, and these included, an interaction between Earth and the black hole at the centre of our galaxy, and the collision of the Earth with a planet called Nibiru. But Mr Clegg was particularly concerned that the United States government believed that when the Earth crossed the middle of the Solar System on that potentially fateful date, that there would be a shift in magnetic poles from the ends of the earth, causing a reversal in accepted scientific principles. We would all no doubt agree that such an outcome would be most worrying.
To this end, and after much discussion over large quantities of the fine Newcastle Exhibition strong ale, available in the House of Commons bar, we agreed to hastily form two essential committees, generously aided by a government grant of £10.5 million.
These committees would be the Conference for Research into Accepted Principles (to been known as CRAP) charged with the responsibility to investigate and experiment, and the Service for the Handling and Interpretation of Terminological Expressions (to been known as SHITE) being the reporting arm of the project.
Time was of the essence, and so to expedite the project we enlisted the help of the very eminent Norwegian Scientist Doctor Yllis Rekcuf and his trusty assistant Laer Dnebonk who have many years' experience of research in this field.

Now, ladies and gentlemen our research portfolio was indeed extensive, and so in the interests of brevity, I propose to deal exclusively here with the main points.

Today I, as the chairman of SHITE, am proud to report, a few of the findings of our CRAP research team.

We at CRAP quickly began to refine our parameters, and to then focus our attention on an investigation into the principles of Upside Down, Back to Front, and Inside Out.

Our first discussion at CRAP centred around the assertion, offered by some members of the committee, that if the world were turned upside down, we in Britain would all be Australian. That our weather would be infinitely better, as would perhaps our beer, but on the down side we would find ourselves eating kangaroo burgers and crocodile sausages. We would be much more successful at cricket, tennis, and other summer sports, but totally inept at International Football. After much debate, it was concluded that as far as football was concerned, the British public would not notice a significant difference.

Secondly, we at CRAP investigated the possibility of gravity turning upside down. It was suggested that this would solve our economic crisis overnight, because all the money would fall out of the rich people's pockets, and if we could develop a mechanism for collecting this money the Exchequer would indeed find itself in an enviable and advantageous position. However, it was pointed out that the money would also fall out of all the poor people's pockets, and therefore this principle would not prove popular with the less wealthy, and in particular the working classes. One interesting effect of the reversal of gravity, which was enthusiastically welcomed by all members of the CRAP committee, was the expectation that at least it might stop raining.

In our 3rd CRAP experiment we set out to prove, that in many circumstances the principle of Upside Down, was effectively the same as Back to Front. This proved fairly easy to determine, and if you will bear with me, I shall with your assistance demonstrate our findings now. Note that my assistant Doctor Rekcuf is at this moment putting my overcoat on me back to front. But having done that if I lie down flat on the floor you will note that my overcoat will indeed be upside down. By applying the simple principle of movement, from a perpendicular to a horizontal position, I can say that the theory is proven beyond any doubt. Now, while Doctor Rekcuf removes my overcoat, let me tell you that this experiment was conducted not only with coats of many types, but also items of clothing worn by men, women and children, and in a few cases by monkeys, chimpanzees, and gorillas. It was found to be proven, when also using shirts, trousers, and cardigans. Interestingly we also discovered at CRAP that if one puts one's underpants on inside out, that they were in principle already upside down, and this was also the case with tights and socks. The back to front/upside down theory was also proven with knickers, and stockings, and I personally can confirm this finding to be absolutely true.

We conducted an enormous range of other experiments, which I regret I do not have the time to outline to you today. So again, ladies and gentlemen in the interests of brevity, and in the certain knowledge that we are all short of time, I shall summarise and conclude with some of our other most significant findings:-

!) We discovered that if all the chips fried on a Friday night in Newcastle were piled up from the Earth to reach the Moon, end to end and upside down, the people of Newcastle would still manage to eat them all.
2) We concluded that if all the actors in the popular television programme The Only Way is Essex with an I Q over 50 were laid end-to-end, either upside down or back to front, on the M25 that there would still be nobody to run over.
3) We tackled the intriguing problem of why, when one drops a piece of toast, it always lands butter side down. We were able to refine through extensive experimentation that toast would never land on its edge and stay there, whether it was laid back to front or upside down. Therefore we resolved that the best way to tackle this problem would be, to either not butter the toast at all, or to butter both sides.
Possibly most interesting of all:
4) We have determined that the growing incidence of homosexuality throughout the world can be explained by an apparent confusion between Front Bottom and Backside.

I am eternally grateful to the British Government and to Nick Clegg in particular, for the generous funding of the CRAP and SHITE project, and their continuing support for crucially important undertakings such as this.

I'm afraid there will be no time for questions, as I have to swiftly make my way to Southampton where my new ocean going yacht is ready to weigh anchor, and to set sail for my new home in Italy. But as I retire to my brand new 20 roomed villa in the foothills of the Tuscany mountain range, I thank you for attending and for listening to our findings.
May I leave you with a very profound thought? It is clear that the principles of Upside Down, Back to Front, and Inside Out

deserve more research. We at CRAP and SHITE have only begun to scratch the surface.
This paper was always, and will remain “etulosba esnesnon“. If you remain unconvinced, and cannot believe me, then please apply the principle of Back to Front to the names of myself and my eminent colleagues.

*The smartly dressed professorial type leaves the stage, to tumultuous applause, and critical acclaim. It is now lunchtime and the men in well-cut suits and power-dressed women, will now tuck into yet another fine feast financed by the public purse.*

## Oh to be an Englishman

***I visited The Lock tearooms at Heybridge Basin to see Martin Newell also known as "The Wild Man of Wivenhoe". It was one of the events for the Essex Book Festival in 2013. He was brilliant! A lot of his poems seemed to be cleverly constructed with quite short and to the point observations. His very informal performance was a true inspiration, and when I came home I wrote this short poem.***

(With thanks to Robert Browning for the inspiration of his first line)

8th March, 2013

Oh to be an Englishman, now that Summer is here,
Sitting in the Red Lion garden, sipping lukewarm beer,
A beer with depth and flavour, that packs a real ale punch,
English cheeses to savour, in my English Ploughman's lunch,
A warm breeze oozing through the trees,
A touch of sunshine on my face,
A hum of buzzing bumble bees,
Summer flowers in full blaze,
The Morris Men in merry dance,
Tradition from afar still near,
Oh to be an Englishman, now that Summer is here.

## Colchester Hospital

***My ex-wife Rosemary was having radiotherapy at Colchester Hospital about 30 miles away, in a schedule of 15 treatments in 3 weeks. The journey was mostly very easy, and the dog Oscar enjoyed the walks around Colchester. The treatment regime was quick and efficient, but the car parking was diabolical. After I'd visited The Lock tearooms at Heybridge Basin to see Martin Newell, I had the inspiration to write this short poem about the experience.***

8th March, 2013

Colchester Hospital, car park too small,
You queue in the rain, by the bin that is full,
With fag ends discarded by the people who won't,
Give up their bad habit, for the people who don't
Want to breathe in the stain, that's polluting their brain.

Car park attendant, stands there and grins,
Inanely, insanely, 'til he guides you in,
To a space he selects, on the visitors row,
As ambulance cars they come and they go,
While you wait there confused, by the man's entry booth.

Radiotherapy, appointments to keep,
Fifteen visits to make, every day for three weeks,
A fifty mile round trip from Chelmsford by car,
To irradiate you, to make sure you are,
Freed from the cursed cells, that dumped you in this hell.

Colchester Hospital, it feels so wrong,
As you drive there and back, taking 4 times as long,
As the fifteen minutes treatment, fifteen minutes of burn,
If only it was fifteen minutes, before you return,
For fifteen minutes lying in that radiated space,
sometimes it takes twice as long to find a parking space.

## Questionnaire

***Christine McDonald, a member of the writer's group, brought this subject matter to the group for homework. It took the form of a list of questions. Most answered them honestly from their personal experience. I decided to play with the questionnaire.***

4th April, 2013

There was a Life Celebration Supper,
where I met a clever young lady,
She said "Hi you look worried,
can I take you over the rainbow?",
You just complete a quick test,
and fill in this short questionnaire,
Then I'll take a look at your answers,
and I'll know if I can take you there.
Somewhere over the rainbow, we could fly,
Somewhere over the rainbow, once in a lullaby.

She said, which hysterical figure would you want to be?
I said, the answer is easy is has to be me.
She asked, what was the first record I ever bought?
And I answered, same as you, my birth certificate,
She said, what is my favourite music at this moment?
I said, right now I really like the sound of silence,
She asked, what's the best book that I've ever read?
And I answered, that has to be the Book of the Dead.

She said, what's my favourite film of all time?
I said, you know cling film sticks in my mind,
She asked, Who were my dream party guests,
dead or alive?
And I answered, it's the Osmonds and dead not alive,
She said, which living person do you admire
and why should it be?
I said, well, isn't that obvious, it has to be me?
She asked, What my friend is your guilty pleasure?
And I answered, Er! I think that could possibly be
procrastination, but can I get back to you on that?

She said, what quality in other people do you admire?
I said, that wealth is the quality to which I aspire,
She asked, what's the most important lesson
life has taught you?
And I answered, that life has taught me
that I'm not immortal,
She said, what superpower would you like to possess?
I said, there's only one superpower,
and that's America I guess,
She asked, what are the most
treasured possessions you prize?
And I answered, that has to be my ears and my eyes.

She said, which people have had
most influence on your life?
I said, that's easy, it's the people who've loved me,
She asked, which pet stands out as extra special?
And I answered, no contest, that has to be Lassie,

She said, what do your consider
your greatest achievement so far?
I said, just staying alive while driving my car,
She asked, what are your wishes for the future honestly?
And I answered, my best wishes that just has to be.

She said, what life questions
do you still have unanswered?
I said, all my life questions are still left unanswered,
She asked, what's the first word
that springs to your mind now?
And I answered, well now that it's over,
it has to be Wow!

When the questionnaire was finished,
I looked at the clever young lady,
She said "It's no surprise to me,
that for you there's no rainbow?",
You've completed this test,

and filled in a short questionnaire,
I've taken a look at all your answers,
But, I'm sorry I can't take you there.
Somewhere over the rainbow, you can't fly,
Somewhere over the rainbow, just wave me goodbye.

Something Else
(A load of rambling nonsense about something other than the colours of the rainbow)

***This free form poem is the result of another Writing Group homework exercise, which adequately describes itself. But perhaps I'm beginning to write rambling poems only loosely associated with the intended subject matter. You decide.***

3rd to 6th May, 2013

I was asked to write a piece to be called something else,
But every time I tried, my thoughts were cast aside,
By an another idea that was languishing on the shelf,
That wouldn't go away, and held me in its sway,
In the grip of a dilemma for day after day.

When I picked up the pen the words would not flow,
And the keyboard just, collected the dust,
Words tangled my fingers the agony lingers,
To resolve this problem I must,
Begin to write what I know, about the colours of the rainbow.

The first idea that I could find, in the dark recesses of my mind,
Was not the ROYGBIV that my memory jars,
So they say Richard of York gave battle in vain,
But what I thought about was green cars,
And how they've taken over from the reds and the blacks,
And possibly the silvers in the future,
They come in many shades, fashioned and made,
In any tint or hint of green that'll suit yer.

So beware of people who drive green cars,
If you'd care to see they strive too far,
To prove their essentials are green and true,
By moving their credentials into my view,
But they still use petrol and diesel too,
Why not, it's good enough for me and you.

Can it really be that to drive a green car
means it's ecologically sound,
If the driver can't see over the steering wheel,
as the other four wheels go round and round,
And if it's electric that totally pathetic,
because
it's actually powered by fossil fuels we're burning,
Yet they wave and they smile, for mile upon mile,
when the wind turbine has stopped turning,
No, beware of people who drive green cars,
Eco warriors they'll claim to be,
Whilst laying the blame for the global warm,
On the likes of you and me.

Now, beware of people who wear brown shoes,
If you'd care to see that it's more bad news,
Leather when tanned is naturally brown,
Whether the cow was standing or laying down.

Beware of people who don red hats,
If you care to see what's wrong with that,
A saying that cannot be ignored,
Suggests a red hat means they're wearing no drawers.

In a world where white elephants are everywhere,
There are pink flamingos and mad March hares,
There are great crested newts and cute little voles,
Blue whales, giant snails, and smooth skinned moles,
The great white shark, and grey Canada geese,
But no blue giraffes, or purple wildebeest.

Now at last to the matter, of the colours of the rainbow,
I'll lay them on a platter, in the order that you know.

Beware of people who wear red hats and shoes,
Red sails in the sunset is much better news,
Steer clear of secret eaters of duck a la'range,
Especially in France, where they don't eat, they mange,
Avoid anybody with a yellow bunch of roses,
I'm leaving you, darling, are the words that it proposes,
As I've said, beware of people, who drive green motors,

Especially those that are Green Party voters,
Don't go dancing with people in blue suede shoes,
And please don't step on them, whatever you do,
Now indigo is something with which you shouldn't bother,
Except in the rainbow there no such colour,
Of people who eat Parma violets you must remain aware,
They've reached the end of the rainbow,
and you don't need to go there,
Even if you're looking for a pot of gold,
You won't find one there, even though it's been foretold.

And so my friends before you go,
There's something else that you should know,
While we've talked of worlds and waterfalls,
And gazed amazed at crystal balls,
And deliberated at rights and wrongs,
And read our books and sung our songs,
In the great realm of things,
In the daily grind,

The Oracle may have changed his mind,
He's concerned that we must surely know,
There's something else before we go,
Here's words of wisdom for you to find,
Exploring colours in my mind.

Little people in a big tree

***A writing group friend, Estella Boxhall-Hutson, bought a cartoon page with people standing, sitting, falling from a big tree, to the writers group. We were asked to use it as inspiration for a piece of writing.***

8th May, 2013

Hello ladies, once again,
Nice to see you now and then,
What's the homework? Can it be?
Little people in a big tree?

The tree looks like a mighty oak, oh my gosh, by golly,
There's little people everywhere,
like a version of Where's Wally?

They are sleeping, they are climbing,
waving, holding hands, and then,
They are standing, they are sitting,
falling, dancing, hanging men.

Estella's tree is a mighty oak, and just as mighty weird,
And what you ladies write about it, I can't wait to hear.

But hasn't the homework gone strange?
Such an immensely diverse range,
Of subject matter to ponder,
Do you ladies remember I wonder,
When we all tried writing villanelles,
An awkwardly structured poetic piece,
Well at least we all had a go.
And then
We came to dangerous curves,
and a man living on his nerves,
A few days in the life of a man with a Porsche,
Now becoming a novel of course.

Then there was a portrait of a punk,
The magic, the madness, and the mystery,
The dignity of the moment,
The holiday, and a dinner party,
This was followed by Upside Down,
And then a Life Celebration Supper
rounded it off with a Questionnaire,
Estella was a cat, I sang a song,
and Christine wasn't there.
So back to the tree, it made me think
of all the different things we've done,
Since we began meeting here at the White Horse,
writing just for fun,
When I look, I try to work out which little man is me,
And after looking for a while, I know which man I'll be,
Top right, on the end of the branch,
sitting down, deep in thought, and yes,
I'll ask of you to tell me,
which little man suits you best?

An Autumn invitation to Halloween Danger Cake
(You need to be careful with that)

***A range of subjects were chosen for a homework exercise. These were, "Autumn", "An Invitation", Halloween", "Danger Cake", and "You need to be careful with that". I decided to write a piece of nonsense verse including all the subjects, and this is the result.***

12th November, 2013

On the 31st of October,
There's an annual young gangster regime,
Of fake zombies rising from their graves,
To celebrate Halloween,
It maybe only one night in the year,
When demons stalk your street,
Dressed up as ghouls or skeletons,
Ready for trick or treat,
But underneath the Asda costume,
Hidden in the folklore bluff and mist,
Is a miniature part time criminal, A trainee terrorist,
That gentle, stage-managed persuasion,
To bribe them with chocolate or sweets,
Well, you know you need to be careful with that,
When they're playing trick or treat,
And it wouldn't do to be saying,
I wish I'd been quicker on my feet,
If only I'd been more careful with that,
When they were playing trick or treat.

When Summer has crashed down to its knees,
And hides behind a rising wall,
The swirling winds and turning leaves,
Bid hello and welcome to the Fall,
Red, gold, and yellow tumbling leaves,
Show Autumn's colourful splash,
A letter box rattles in the wind,
As a wily fox raids dustbin trash,
Warm overcoats are dusted off,
With scarves, and hats, and gloves,

As icy rain comes lashing down,
From the angry grey skies above,
Quick season's clock goes ticking by,
To measure out it's changing ways,
Well, you know you need to be careful with that,
And treasure every one of your passing days,
And it wouldn't do to be saying,
I wish I'd been more wise in my ways,
If only I'd been more careful with that,
And treasured every one of my days,

When we had barbecues in the gardens,
And enjoyed black chargrilled food,
Had picnics in the primrose wood,
Went swimming in the nude,
Had birthday party bouncy castles,
And wedding reception celebrations,
Funeral wakes with fancy cakes,
And graduation invitations,
There were Valentine’s Day flowers,
And Easter Eggs and Bunnies were found,
Boxes of chocs, and novelty socks,
When Christmastime came around,
But I'm not sure about this strange invite
If this kind of bash is really for me,
Well, you know you need to be careful with that,
I've never been to a that kind of party,
And it wouldn't do to be saying,
I wish I'd been not quite so flash
If only I'd been more careful with that,
Invite to a swinger's bash.

She stood in the kitchen completely alone,
Comfortably dressed in a onesy,
She had a request to do her best,
To bake some currant bunsy,
That definitely wasn't her forte,
She had better things to make,
It was nicer to be naughty,
And to arrange for a danger cake,
All the ingredients were assembled,

And she started to mix and to bake,
And added that extra secret touch,
That's essential for danger cake,
You're going to be taking your life in your hands,
You may vanish without a trace,
Well, you know you need to be careful with that,
In case it explodes in your face,
And it wouldn't do to be saying,
Why I only had one slice,
If only I'd been more careful with that,
But danger cake's far too nice.

## An Englishman Abroad

***If you've been anywhere on the Costas then you'll know precisely what this piece is all about. It became a song which was recorded at Highfield Studios on the CD album, "And the Band Played On" in 2016.***

21st November, 2013

On a foreign field that is for never England,
He sits outside the Queen Vic bar in the Spanish sun,
Watching repeats of Premier League football on the telly,
And reading yesterday's issue of the Currant Bun.

Lager, lager, lager is his battle cry, his raison d'être,
It really is all for him and none for all,
He's a great fat twerp in a multi-coloured shirt,
Who does a bomb and empties half the pool.

Oh, there's nothing worse than the eternal curse
of the Englishman abroad,
He's a loud-mouthed lout,
with a lager snout,
who will not be ignored,
He spouts his Rule Britannia views,
his Land of Hope and Glory song,
He's a Philistine with a fractured mind,
who really can't tell right from wrong.

When lunchtime comes around and he gets peckish,
He ain't gonna go for none of that foreign muck,
It's chips and burgers and lashings of Colman's mustard,
He's a Philistine and he doesn't give a f**k.

For paella, and tortillas, and olives, and all that crap,
He surely wouldn't give you the time of day,
Just wrap in up in a St Georges flag and baseball cap,
And drop him in the depths of San Antonio Bay.

Oh, there's nothing worse than the eternal curse
of the Englishman abroad,
He's a loud-mouthed lout,
with a lager snout,
who will not be ignored,
He spouts his Rule Britannia views,
his Land of Hope and Glory song,
He's a Philistine,
with a fractured mind,
who really can't tell right from wrong.

The culture and history of the Nation he is visiting,
The people and their customs can be ignored,
They really are of absolutely no consequence at all,
It's a shame for them that they're not
an Englishman abroad.

So if you meet this hero of the revolution,
While you're holidaying in Espana by the foam,
You'll maybe wonder why you really bothered,
It might have been much better to stay at home.

Oh, there's nothing worse than the eternal curse
of the Englishman abroad,
He's a loud-mouthed lout,
with a lager snout,
who will not be ignored,
He spouts his Rule Britannia views,
his Land of Hope and Glory song,
He's a Philistine with a fractured mind,
who really can't tell right from wrong.

# CHAPTER 6

## And the Band Played On

***"Each life is just another song,***
***A rhythm and a melody,***
***Some words you sing in harmony,***
***And even if the tune is wrong,***
***If you're singing in a different key,***
***Still in the end it's clear to see,***
***Whether the ride was short or long,***
***The band still played on."***

The eyes follow you around the room
(Originally titled "The Painting")

***This was an exercise to write something called "The Painting". Having googled a number of well-known portraits like La Giaconda, The Scream, and the Laughing Cavalier, I came across a discussion between two art critics about the background to the most famous painting in the World, and decided to write a short story featuring that. I fail to see how anyone could not be fascinated by Leonardo da Vinci, and his legendary superpowers, so he had a big part to play. Once I started writing this just flowed off the pen, or should I say dripped from my three typing figures onto the keyboard.***

20/27th January, 2014

Lenny Davin put the phone down after saying, "I'm so grateful Lucas. Thank you so much. I'll be in touch soon."
He paced up and down, couldn't relax. It was a good job he had a huge spacious apartment otherwise he would have been in danger of wearing a long bare patch in the plush carpet. It was July, and air-conditioning was working at full blast, otherwise the sweltering New York weather, and traffic noise would have been unbearable. Lenny had lived in the Big Apple all his life and his swish warehouse apartment for over 15 years. He loved New York, its hustle and bustle, its orderly untidiness, its brutally different seasons, and its brash, get-out-of-my-way-I'm-too-busy-for-you attitude. As a celebrity photographer it had been good to him, brought him wealth and status. He had taken photographs of Presidents, Royalty, and major celebrities. At 65 he was in pretty good shape for native New Yorker.
He looked at his ornate clock a miniature version of the clock in Grand Central Station. It was 8.05 pm. Half an hour that's all, and he would have the document that Lucas Protheroe had been putting together for him for more than 5 years. He had never been so nervous, so excited, so wound up like a coiled spring. He'd let the concierge know to bring the package straight up to number 174 when the motorcycle courier delivered it. Now all he could do was wait, and pace up and down, up and down wearing a groove in the carpet.
"Thirty-five minutes! Where in the name of Sam Hill is that

delivery boy?" he asked himself out loud, and then he went on, "Calm down! Calm down boy! You've waited for years, and a few minutes more won't make any difference."
Reassuring himself didn't stop him being on edge. He took a look out of the huge panoramic window, saw the traffic in the streets below snarling around in its usual patterns, traffic lights on red and green, Walk and Don't Walk!, yellow cabs, delivery trucks, buses, 2 million people all moving with purpose in different directions.
"Ding Dong, Ding Dong!" the doorbell rang. His feet didn't touch the ground as he rushed across the room to open the door.
"Package for you Mr Davin." said the concierge handing over a big brown envelope.
"Thanks Johnny." he replied giving him the 5 dollar bill he'd been rolling around in his fist for nearly 40 minutes.
He sat down in his Bloomingdales luxury armchair, and breathed a big sigh. He looked at the package, and now he had it in his hand he wanted to savour the moment before opening it. It only took seconds to reflect the long road that he'd travelled to get to this moment in his life. He knew that some of what Protheroe had written for him would already be his common knowledge, but somewhere in amongst all of the ordinary stuff there would be some stones overturned with surprises lurking underneath. He began reading.
For the first 30 minutes it was all stuff he had embedded in him like his own DNA. How his grandparents had emigrated to America from Florence, Italy in 1921, and arrived along with all the other hopefuls at Ellis Island Immigration Post looking for a better life. He remembered how his grandfather had told him all about the journey, for weeks getting to Hamburg in Germany and then across the Atlantic, and how thousands of people were quickly processed on arrival to be allowed into the New World. Papa Carlo, as he called him had told the story how many people left Europe with their real name and were quickly registered in America with a new truncated name. He was told about a friend he'd made on the voyage, who left Lithuania as Stanislaus Brzchinesvsky and discovered America as Stanley Birzin. Everybody had their names adulterated for the sake of efficiency and to meet the immigration clerks processing quotas. The document Protheroe had produced illustrated the family line going further back through the generations. He had done a

marvellous, precise and meticulously detailed job putting this work together. Lenny was getting deeper and deeper into his family tree. He studied each line carefully, where his ancestors lived in little villages like Anchiano around the City of Florence, births, christenings, marriages, deaths, occupations, through 20 generations. It took him hours as he pored over and absorbed every little detail. The task filled him with an overwhelming awareness of who he was and how he had come to be.
He was so immersed in his personal history he hardly noticed that nearly 4 hours had dissolved as easily as cubes of sugar in his coffee cup. But the photographer felt he had to get to the crunch, the raison d' être for all the expensive and time-consuming research that the best genealogist in America, if not the World, had done for him. And he wasn't just going to skip to the bottom line. No! He wanted to get there by savouring every moment, every nuance, and every little detail.
It was gone midnight. He took a deep breath, went to the kitchen and poured himself a beer, and then settled back down in the armchair. "Only 3 generations to go." he told himself.
An hour later and there it was. The proof! He grinned, and felt an electric pulse of extreme satisfaction move through him like a warm comfortable wave breaking on a sun-baked shore. It was confirmed. He was a direct descendant of the great man; some say the most intelligent man who has ever lived, the brilliant painter, sculptor, architect, musician, mathematician, engineer, inventor, anatomist, geologist, cartographer, botanist, and writer, Leonardo da Vinci. Leonardo di ser Piero da Vinci, born 15th April 1452 and died 2nd May 1519. Born out-of-wedlock, son of the wealthy Messer Piero Fruosino di Antonio da Vinci, a Florentine legal notary, and Caterina, a peasant girl.
That was what he wanted. That was what he had paid Protheroe to find out. Now he knew why he Lenny Davin was such a brilliant photographer. He shared some genes with his ancestor, an understanding of composition, light and shade, colour, shadow, foreground, background, expression. Delighted was not the word to describe where he was at that moment in time.
It was late, and he went to bed, fulfilled, ecstatic, feeling that the whole of his life had been leading up to that moment of discovery.

But he was exhausted after ploughing through the document. He didn't sleep well. The excitement of the previous few hours had his mind on a razor's edge, and soon his big windows were letting in the brightness of another New York day. He got up moving in a strange, floating way towards his armchair, and picked up the Protheroe document again. Maybe it was the lack of sleep, and his tired eyes, but he kicked himself because in his haste to open the envelope he had missed something the previous night. A large paper-clip held another smaller envelope to the back of the family tree document that he had perused so carefully. On it Protheroe had written:

"My Dear Friend,

Don't open this until you are sure you want the whole truth.

This is dangerous stuff!

Regards Lucas Protheroe"

Lenny felt sick. He went to the bathroom, and then into the kitchen to fix his breakfast, Columbian coffee, Florida orange juice, toast and Scottish marmalade. He wondered what that 2nd envelope would reveal. AS was his morning habit he switched on the massive flat screen TV, and tuned into a world news channel.

"Breaking news this morning from our news agency in Rome reports that the world famous genealogist Lucas Protheroe had been found dead in suspicious circumstances in his hotel room. He had been staying in the Hotel Palazzo Montemartini.
Mr Protheroe had been in Italy for nearly 3 years doing research work at many places in and around Florence, and in the Vatican archives. We'll update you on this report when we get more."

The New Yorker was stunned.
"What in the name of Sam Hill is going on?" he asked himself, and "What does Protheroe mean that this stuff is dangerous?" His toast stuck in his gullet, his coffee didn't want to go down. He felt even more sick. He played with the envelope, turning it over and over in his trembling hands. He put it down, picked it up again, turned it over and over again, read the words on the front again 3 or 4 times.

"What can it be?" he asked himself, "It's not Pandora's box. It's just an envelope for Christ sakes."
He stared into space for a while trying to focus his mind on opening, or destroying, or maybe handing the envelope over to the police.
"So Protheroe is dead! Maybe I owe it to him to find out why, if the clues are in this envelope." he told himself.
He steeled himself and slid his finger in the side to rip open the enclosure, took a deep breath and began reading.

> "Oh Dear Lenny,
>
> You are indeed a brave and possibly foolhardy man. But my friend I have to tell you that no harm will come to you if you stop reading now, and destroy what you have in your hand. The consequences if you read on are unpredictable, for you may have the future of America, the World, and the human race in your hands."

This was Protheroe giving him a final chance, but Lenny had come this far and now he wasn't going to turn back. Something came back to him from his teenage years when he had heard a song called From the Underworld by a group called the Herd. The lyric was based on a story from Greek mythology. He liked it so much he had committed it to memory. The words were ringing in his ears as his tortured mind told him to go and read on.

> **"Out of the land of shadows and darkness,**
> **We were returning towards the morning light,**
> ..........................................................................
> **Into another world you entered and**
> **never again I can reclaim you."**

The song echoed around his brain distracting him from the task ahead. Then he took another deep breath, and read on. Protheroe had written:

"For five years I toiled away on this work for you, in the States, through Europe, and finally into Italy, and it was indeed a fascinating piece of research. In the end I had to get permission from the Vatican to examine manuscripts hidden away since the early 1500's. Written in Latin at a time when most of the population were illiterate, Columbus had only just discovered America, and most scholars and theologists still believed the World was flat; this was painstaking work to analyse and interpret. But here goes. Brace yourself for a shock.

It was known that from September 1513 to 1516, under Pope Leo X, da Vinci spent much of his time living in the Belvedere in the Vatican in Rome. It was assumed that this was solely for him to undertake artistic projects for the Papacy, but I've discovered that isn't entirely true. The Papal Council were concerned that La Giaconda, better known nowadays as the Mona Lisa which it is claimed Leonardo painted between 1503 and 1507 illustrated some disturbing issues. The famous enigmatic smile being one, the way the eyes are set is another, but most worrying of all to the church elders was the background to the portrait which seemed to be "Of another World!"

In addition it was of concern to the authorities where their guest had acquired his engineering knowledge. In 1502 he produced a drawing of single span 720-foot bridge as part of a civil engineering project for Ottoman Sultan Beyazid II of Constantinople. He had also drawn up plans for 2 flying machines, the helical rotor and the ornithopter.

So basically the High Church establishment were undermined and disturbed by his intelligence and how he had acquired it. They wanted to maintain a vice-like grip on all matters of knowledge or intelligence, and da Vinci was potentially a dangerous heretic. The manuscripts revealed evidence that while he was in the Belvedere he was tortured and eventually confessed that he had been abducted by aliens in May 1503, and had painted his most famous work La Giaconda, the Mona Lisa, while on planet Zaegafor 19, which is 37.2 light years from Earth

At the same time as da Vinci had been stolen from the Earth the Zaegafori had kidnapped a Florentine woman for the sole purpose of improving their bloodline. They became friends during their abduction and she is the subject of the painting of La Giaconda. Her smile reflects the exceptionally friendly treatment she was afforded by both da Vinci and her alien captors. The background to the most famous painting in the World is other worldly because quite simply the artist and his sitter were both on another world when it was painted.

The aliens were super intelligent and highly advanced compared to their Earthly subjects. But at that time they were not hostile. In fact they enjoyed da Vinci's superior Earthly intellect, almost as much as they enjoyed the Florentine woman. Their male visitor was so trusted by them that they allowed him access to their archives and libraries. So while the earthly genius was on Zaegafor 19 he took the opportunity to study and copy the concepts he would employ for the Constantinople Bridge and the 2 flying machines. Despite his intellect he got them both slightly wrong."

Lenny stopped reading at that point and reflected on what he had just learned. It was indeed an amazing and unbelievable revelation. But had he got to anything that could be marked as dangerous? It made him feel quite special that his ancient ancestor had been to another planet and consorted with aliens, and he fully understood why the Vatican wouldn't want this information to be common knowledge. It put the Catholic Church and the concept of One God on shaky foundations.

He read on.

"So now you know my friend that you are direct descendant of Leonardo da Vinci, and you know perhaps why he was such a brilliant and intelligent man. But his abduction has a sting in the tail, because the aliens only agreed to transport him and the woman back to Earth, and to allow the painting of the Mona Lisa to go back with them, with one certain very precise condition. And that was that from that point on in World history, starting with that masterpiece every painting subsequently produced would have eyes that seemed to follow the observer around the room. And the reason they do that my friend is that we are all being monitored. Those eyes are all like very advanced CCTV cameras.
WE ARE ALL BEING WATCHED BY MEN FROM OUTER SPACE, and when they feel the time is right for them they will come and get us.
In addition da Vinci learned that the Zaegafori had throughout their history kidnapped species from other worlds, and assimilated their genes into their own bloodline. This was always a prelude to a benign invasion where the products of the species

mixture would gradually take over the chosen planet. The gestation period for this plan to eventually populate the entire Universe was set as 1.3 treppia. This measurement was calculated by our Florentine mathematician as approximately 511.7 Earth years. Lenny, my friend, do the sums. 1503 add 511.7 years given a reasonable margin for error means that any day now............................."

One of those awful nights

***Project - A 10 minute moment in terms of the senses" (sight, sound, smell, touch, taste, + thoughts and feelings). Sorry, but it took quite a bit more than 10 minutes.***

21st March, 2014

It happens every now and again,
And I'm having one of those awful nights,
Sleep elusive, sheer frustration,
Has me in its clutches tight.

An impenetrable wall of insomniac dry fog,
Surrounding me and choking,
Like an invisible blanket suffocating,
My mouth and lips are dry as sandpaper,
My tongue like leather pizza,
My Sahara mouth tastes only salty cardboard.

The dim orange street lights are clever imposters,
They should be comforting and softer,
But they sear through my eyelids, and scar
my tired eyeballs like the floodlights at Wembley stadium.

Check the clock, What is the time?
Tell myself "I should be fast asleep by now."
Must get some shut-eye, don't know how.

The bed mattress is a great pretender,
A soft and comfy surface to aid my rest,
But it seems to undulate like a conveyor belt,
A corrugated iron rack under my back.

My memory foam pillow irritates,
It is Ayer's Rock under my head and neck,
And it whispers constantly, taunting words,
"You're not sleeping, Ha! Ha! Ha!
You're not sleeping, Ha! Ha! Ha!"
Taunting words, spinning around my brain,
Teasing, bullying, again and again.

Smell the freshness in the air,
Feel the tension, hanging there,
Smell the rain, hear the traffic, hear a train,
Loud and louder, hear the rain.

Am I too warm, or am I too cold,
Did I lock the door, did I close the window,
Check the gas and taps are off,
Am I going slowly mad,
Or am I just getting old?

Check the clock, What is the time?
Tell myself "I should be fast asleep by now."
Must get some shut-eye, don't know how.

Desperation envelopes me, what can I do?
Try to keep calm, try deep breathing,
Reciting rhymes, singing songs,
Search memory banks for places to relax,
OK, I'm on the beach at Montego Bay,
Visualise, sun shining, waves lapping the shore,
That's better, Oh what a relief,
Feel myself, drifting off to sleep,
At last, ah peace, perfect peace.

Whoosh! Then a javelin hits my brain,
Breaks my drift with an arresting jolt,
Immediate thoughts, insistent thoughts,
persistent thoughts,
Deal with me now thoughts,
You're not daring to go to sleep are you? thoughts,
Back to square one, wide awake again.

Wonder what the time is now?
Take another look at that damn clock,
Only minutes passing oh so slowly,
Shall I get up and make camomile tea?

I can't escape, it won't let me go my way,
The arms of Morpheus would be so welcome,
But they are so remote, so far away.
Leave me alone, let me be,
I want your evil grip to release me,
Leave me in peace,
Please, please, please,
Let me go to sleep,
Let me go to sleep.

And the Band Played On

***I started writing this piece on 16th March 2014.***
***The brief was simply to write something; a story, poem, or song called "And the band played on".***
***From the beginning I knew it had to be a song.***
***The usual way I construct any song is to write a poem and then set it to music. But that really is an over-simplification of the whole process.***
***Whenever I write a song initially I will write out the first few words, lines, or ideas by hand, and it may be a long time before I commit something to the keyboard and computer.***

***For this piece I've outlined the process I followed from start to finish.***

***Phase 1 - Sow the seed***

***The opening thoughts were that the song should use "the Band" as a metaphor for how our lives are just a brief interlude, and how the world goes on before and after us regardless. The most constant part of a tune any band plays is probably the drumbeat, and so that gets a big part in my early thinking. On the 16th March then, I scribbled down 2 verses:***

"The war was over, and the boys were heading homeward,
Medals awarded, straight lines moving forward,
In the celebration of victory, or humiliation of defeat,
The drums still echoed out to an incessant beat,
all along the street.

The last show closed down at the end of the pier,
Washed away like the sands on the beach, no longer here,
The aroma of the cigarette butts, and lukewarm, flat beer,
Leaves the drummer's hands silenced in the cold atmosphere."

***I'm not thinking about meter at this stage, or fitting words to a tune here, just getting the ideas down. On 17th March, I added 2 more verses:***

"The last waltz was danced, and the party was done,
All the balloons had been burst at the end of the fun,
The battles for lust had been lost or been won,
By soon broken promises for the moon and the sun.

The final breath was tasted and the heart beat no more,
All eyes were cast downwards to stare at the floor,
On the inside the Big Man threw the bolts on the door,
You stood on the outside, another pebble on the shore,
And the drums have been muffled in name of the law,
While the great scorer comes to tot up your score,
You wonder what in Heaven's name was all the struggle for."

***I woke up on the morning of the 18th March with the words I had written on my mind, and it occurred to me that the whole thing would be better if I injected some personalities into it. So I came up with two lovers called Charlie and Chloe, and began to change the emphasis of the words to include these 2 characters.***
***This would have the effect of turning statements of what happened into a real story rather than a news report.***
***It was at that time that I picked up the guitarand began to doodle with the tune."***

***"Phase 2 - Nurturing the seedling***

***When I start to formulate a tune that will get the meter of the poem going properly. So words get moved around, replaced, discarded and changed to fit the development of a rhythm and a melody. The story is a bit of a sad tale, so the music has to start in a minor key. In this case its a pretty simple E minor and D major sequence for lines 1, 2 and 4, and with each 3rd line providing a contrast and a lift by moving to C major, and then D major, back to C major and returning to E minor.***
***Once the music is on the way the true mood of the piece becomes clear to me. So during that process, the words became:"***

"When Charlie's war was over, and the medals were awarded,
Brave boys all heading homeward, in straight lines going

forward,
In celebration of victory, or humiliation of defeat,
The incessant drum was echoing all along the street.".

"Then Chloe's last show closed down,
in the theatre at the end of the pier,
Washed away like the sands on the beach, gone, no longer here,
There's just the stench of cigarettes, and sickly, lukewarm beer,
And the drums will not be silenced, in the cruel, cold atmosphere."
The Rhyming scheme was now set as either

***A, A, B, B or A, A, A, A for the verses.***

***Once those 2 verses had come together,
I needed to think about a chorus.***

***Phase 3 - Developing the flowerbed***

***Classic song construction a la Tin Pan Alley revolves around a verse, chorus, verse, chorus, bridge, verse, chorus, chorus framework.
That's not a hard and fast rule, but it's also not a bad idea.
And if a song starts in a minor key, it's quite common to move to a major key for the chorus, so that you get some kind of uplift in the mood.
A lot of songs work around the premise that the verses tell a story; they are the narrative, and the chorus provides a resolution or bold statement to contrast.
So, I needed a bold statement that basically sows the seed for "The band being the world going on before you arrive, and after you've gone.", and "Each life" being just a temporary, but totally valid overlay, on the pattern of the world. My first attempt at a chorus had the words:"***

"Each life is just another song, a rhythm and a melody,
Some lyrics and a harmony,
And at the end it's easy to see,
That even if the tune is wrong, In a difficult key or just too long,
The band still plays on, Yes! the band plays on."

***Again, here all I'm doing is getting the ideas on paper. I'm not worrying about meter or fitting them to the music. At that stage I know the natural key for the chorus is going to be G major, because that's the major associated with E minor. The rest of the chords develop from there.***
***Now that the overall idea is beginning to take shape, it's time to transfer the words and chords to the song to keyboard and computer. After I've got a pattern for both words and music, I start to fit other verses into that pattern.***

As a result verses 3 and 4 are transformed to:"

"When the lovers danced their last waltz,
and the party was all done,
All the balloons had been deflated,
burst and broken just for fun,
All the battles for true love were lost,
only greed and lust had won,
Through the triumph and the tragedy,
the drumbeat still went on".

"When Charlie's heart stopped beating,
and so he breathed no more,
Chloe's cast her eyes straight downwards,
staring blankly at the floor,
She cried with pain so deep inside,
as she stood behind the door,
Charlie was trapped on the outside now,
just another pebble on the shore."

***This process develops some of the ideas and discards some others, but ensures a better focus on the subject so that the story then becomes more consistent.***
***Now I stick with what I've written, and start to develop the music side. After a while I've invented a 2 chord musical hook to introduce at stages in the song to pull the listener back to a theme. The chorus is eventually rewritten as:***

"Each life is just another song,
A rhythm and a melody,
some words you sing in harmony,

And even if the tune is wrong,
If you're singing in a different key,
still in the end it's clear to see,
Whether the ride was short or long,
The band still played on."

***The rhyming scheme for the chorus is:-
A, B, B, A, B, B, A, A.***

***Phase 4 - Watering the hanging basket***

***For a few days I played the song as formulated at that stage, but I wasn't satisfied that the words said everything they needed to say, and I didn't have a bridge. A bridge isn't essential, but it does provide another explanatory aspect to the song. After some more development I find another verse, and then a bridge. So on 22nd March I add both of them in.***

***The verse is:"***

"Then Chloe's world was broken,
and she lived inside her head,
Not another word was spoken,
there was nothing to be said,
She drifted through a wilderness,
till her lifeblood dripped no more,
Charlie welcomed her with open arms,
when they met on Heaven's shore."

And the bridge is:-

"This band has been playing in time
since the dawn of creation,
Your ticket for the show lets you go to one destination,
You take chances, make choices,
for distractions, and for excursions,
You get kicked in the teeth with detours,
delays and diversions,
One day you find your time is up,

and there's nowhere else to go,
There's no more succour in your cup,
there's nothing more to know,
The scenes were written just for you,
and you played them from the heart,
And the band will go on playing now,
long after you depart,
And the band played on."

***The bridge has a different poetic construction, and as the 3rd musical element uses another minor key.***
***This time it's A minor. But the tune resolves back to E minor throughout.***
***The rhyming scheme for the bridge is:-***
***A, A, B, B, C, C, D, D, E.***

***By this time I have probably played the piece in its entirety about 20 times.***
***Over the next few days I break up the original bridge, steal 2 lines from it, and construct another verse, all in the name of making sense and completing the story.***
***The additional verse and fade out (coda) ending becomes:"***

"And when the fateful day arrives,
for totting up the score,
Maybe you'll be wondering,
what was all the struggle for,
But the scenes were written just for you,
and you played them from the heart,
And the band will go on playing now,
long after you depart.

And the band played on,
And the band played on,
And the band played on."

By 28th March the work is finished.

***Phase 5 Harvesting the crop.***

***Finally the song has a pattern of:***

***Verse, Verse, Chorus, Verse, Verse, Chorus, Verse, Bridge, Verse, Coda.***
***The musical hook comes in at the beginning, after each chorus, and at the end.***
***So now I've told the story of Charlie coming back from the war, Chloe no longer dancing in the theatre, and told you "That's life!" Then I had them as lovers, touched on their short lives, killed Charlie off, and told you how Chloe felt, before repeating the sentiment "That's the way it goes. Sorry!"***
***Then I had a happy ending with them meeting again on "Heaven's shore" before returning to the theme of the "Band playing on" in the bridge. Finally I bring you personally into the song, by teasing you with "But the scenes were written just for you, and you played them from the heart."***
***Then the song fades with a repetition of "And the band played on".***
***Here's the completed work:-***

And the band played on

16th to 28th March, 2014

When Charlie's war was over,
and the medals were awarded,
Brave boys all heading homeward,
in straight lines going forward,
In celebration of victory, or humiliation of defeat,
The incessant drum was echoing, all along the street.

Then Chloe's last show closed down,
in the theatre at the end of the pier,
Washed away like the sands on the beach,
gone, no longer here,
There's just the stench of cigarettes,
and sickly lukewarm beer,
And the drums will not be silenced,
by the cruel, cold atmosphere.

Each life is just another song,

A rhythm and a melody,
some words you sing in harmony,
And even if the tune is wrong,
If you're singing in a different key,
still in the end it's clear to see,
Whether the ride was short or long,
The band still played on.

When the lovers danced their last waltz,
and the party was all done,
All the balloons had been deflated,
burst and broken just for fun,
All the battles for true love were lost,
only greed and lust had won,
Through the triumph and the tragedy,
the drumbeat still went on.

When Charlie's heart stopped beating,
and so he breathed no more,
Chloe's cast her eyes straight downwards,
staring blankly at the floor,
She cried with pain so deep inside,
as she stood behind the door,
Charlie was trapped on the outside now,
just another pebble on the shore.

Each life is just another song,
A rhythm and a melody,
some words you sing in harmony,
And even if the tune is wrong,
If you're singing in a different key,
still in the end it's clear to see,
Whether the ride was short or long,
The band still played on.

Then Chloe's world was broken,
and she lived inside her head,
Not another word was spoken,
there was nothing to be said,
She drifted through a wilderness,
till her lifeblood dripped no more,

Charlie welcomed her with open arms,
when they met on Heaven's shore.

This band has been playing in time
since the dawn of creation,
Your ticket for the show lets you go to one destination,
You take chances, make choices,
for distractions and for excursions,
You get kicked in the teeth with detours,
delays and diversions,
One day you find your time is up,
and there's nowhere else to go,
There's no more succour in your cup,
there's nothing more to know.

And when the fateful day arrives,
for totting up your score,
Maybe you'll be wondering,
what was all the struggle for,
But the scenes were written just for you,
and you played them from the heart,

And the band will go on playing now,
long after you depart.

And the band played on,
And the band played on,
And the band played on.

Softly (my soul, my heart, my dreams, my love)

***This piece was inspired by an acquaintance of a friend, Christine MacDonald, who wrote the first verse. I reused the pattern in another three verses, and moved from "soul" through to "heart, my dreams, and my love". The key word of the poem is 'softly'.***

10th June, 2014

My soul is like black cat,
it stalks through the darkness of its lair,
Noiseless, on velvet paws,
It can neither be heard nor seen,
but often I can feel it,
As it brushes softly, noiseless,
sensually past my intellect.

My heart is like a red deer,
it leaps highest when in despair,
Graceful, on feather hooves,
It can either be stopped nor stilled,
but often I can feel it,
As it beats softly, graceful, steadily past my mortality.

My dreams are like a dragonfly,
they float through the morning of my thoughts,
Fragile, on delicate wings,
They can neither be touched nor trapped,
but often I can see them,
As they take shape, softly, fragile,
streaming through my imagination.

My love is like your guardian angel,
always looking out for you,
Steadfast, in invisible circles,
It can neither be captured nor imprisoned,
but often I can show it,
As it enfolds you softly, steadfast, and forever true.

Thank You. No!

***Doesn't everybody get thoroughly fed up with junk mail? It's an invasion of your territory and your mind. It's persistent, irritating and mostly unnecessary, because it goes straight in the bin without even a first look. Then there's the unavoidable repetition of television adverts trying in banal and pathetic terms to flog you things you don't need, or wouldn't buy anyway without thorough investigation. And, Oh my God, then there's the same process for television programmes.***

1st June, 2014

While I've been away from home my space has been invaded by a pernicious little character called the postman. He understands that my weak spot is a little flap in my front door called the letter box, and he has no hesitation in making almost daily use of it. So when I return home there on my doorstep are the results of the postman's endeavours. Sometimes, seldom in fact, his deposits on my mat are good news. Most of the time, if they have any true relevance to my life, they are bills illustrating that I owe some organisation money. Strangely I don't really mind any of that. But what does irritate me is the other stuff.
Leaflets! Piles of bloody leaflets, every bloody day.
Do I want a pizza to go, from Domino?
Do I want a takeaway curry from yet another new Indian restaurant that's recently taken over an ailing pub?
Do I want a different broadband provider, like Talk Talk or Plusnet, and why do BT bombard me with information about fibre optics when I'm clearly quite happy with my copper wire Wi-Fi?
Do I have any need of yet more insurance from Direct Line, or some company that wants to bet me that I'm going to die, but in the process of getting there, is convinced that I'll just quietly hand over a wodge of cash to them?
Does the double glazing company know that I live in a cave, and don't have any windows?
Does the solar panel company know that caves don't have roofs?
Why does every bank want to offer me another credit card with an extortionate APR?

Why does MY BANK not check their records before they offer me a credit card that I've already got?
Why do Saga think that I can afford to go on one of their cruise holidays costing £4,000?
There is only one answer to these invasions of my space. Straight in the recycling bin is where they go, with a very polite, and restrained, Thank You. No!

While I'm at home, there's a very clever technical device that has a persuasive grasp on my attention. It sits in the corner and lures me daily to pay homage. Some of the time the TV is interesting and educational, but increasingly it has become a hole in the world that serves up continuous crap. I often ask myself was it better when we only had 5 channels, of even 2?
Now we've got hundreds of channels all serving up the TV equivalent of MacDonald's Big Mac and Fries.
Who in their right mind watches Big Brother?
How many times do we all want to see people eating cockroaches on I'm a Celebrity, pay me loads of money, and I'll sit in the jungle being obnoxious for 2 weeks, while being starved, and surrounded by rats and spiders.
Why is everybody on Eastenders so bloody miserable? Real Eastenders are cheerful and intelligent.
When did Emmerdale morph from a wholesome story about farms, sheep, and bread making, into a sordid tale of bed hopping, cheating, and subterfuge?
How long will it be before I'm selected to be a contestant on Come Dine with Me?
Why is it that every bed and breakfast establishment on Four in a Bed thinks it's reasonable to charge £200 a night?
Why is the weather forecast always more wrong on BBC?
When will one of the programmes featuring people getting drunk on a Saturday night, fighting in the streets, and peeing and puking up in any available corner come to Chelmsford?
Is it a fact that I've already seen all the movies that are worth watching several times, and there really is nothing new to show me but more gruesome violence, more explicit sex, and more car chases.
Do I want to watch About a Boy, My Beautiful Launderette, or Carry on Osama bin Laden again and again and again?
I know who shot J.R. and I know who killed Tina in Coronation

Street (I think, watch this space), but who murdered Bruce Forsyth and replaced him with a hologram?
So most of the time TV is just background noise like a placebo to fill the silence. Do I watch it?
Thank You. No!

Ah but isn't it distressing to find to find that sometimes, only sometimes, the TV advertisements are better than the programmes? That doesn't apply all the time of course.
Why do Virgin and Sky spend so much money trying to persuade me to subscribe to their TV systems? Surely a fair proportion of the people watching are already using them.
Why is it that if I send £2 to Africa they can have fresh water, when it costs me about £300 a year?
Why do I need a Stannah Stairlift when I live in a cave, and don't have stairs?
If Ian Botham goes for a walk so often why does he need Revitive?
Why don't all the football referees at Chelmsford City's matches go to Specsavers?
Has Michael Parkinson got life insurance from the company he wants me to use?
How many mistreated donkeys are there being illegally imported into Britain? Will they take our jobs, and nick our women?
Has Britain been secretly invaded by UKip voting Russian immigrant meerkats?
Why do they keep showing me starving children in Africa just as I'm sitting down to eat?
Why don't the governments of the countries in Africa where the children are starving feed their people, instead of buying guns and mining for uranium?
Do I take any notice of the adverts? Obviously I do, otherwise I wouldn't have said this. But do I buy any of the products advertised? Thank You. No!

So you've probably guessed by now, that my favourite TV programme is "Grumpy Old Men", and I don't have much sentiment for being treated like an idiot, or being regarded as a soft touch for any old charity.
The milk of human kindness has soured in the jug,
The sweet taste of charity has vanished in the fug,

I'm a product of the media, an average man in the street,
But most of all I'd like to think I'm nobody's mug.
So to all that modern chewing gum, throw away after use,
disposable disposables world I say,
Thank You. No!
Thank You. No!
And that's all I've got to say.

## The Nature of Reality

***There must have been something going on that caused me to want to write a little story about fleas. No! I certainly was not scratching around.***

21st July, 2014

Sylvia and Derek (Sylv and Del) were the perfect couple. They had been together for ages. Del was a good looker, a bit of an athlete, and Sylv was no slouch either. They had a beautiful home, snug in a warm fold in the land, and they had many friends and relatives.

It was Friday evening, another Friday evening, and Sylv was at home tidying up as usual while Del had gone off to his favourite watering hole. That night she dined alone. This was becoming a regular occurrence as Del seemed to go off for a drink at the same place almost every day just lately. The sun was just about to set in a big red sky when Del came home, bounding along with that bouncy joyful stride.

"Hi, Honey, I'm home." he smiled.

"Yes, I can see that." she sighed.

"Oh, don't be like that, sweetheart," he turned on the charm, "I've missed you."

"Derek," she said, "I'm fed up, I don't know why you keep going to the nasty end of town, to that shithole, when there's a perfectly good place just around the corner, over that little hill. It's much nicer there, and you know I'll even come with you."

"Sylv, darlin' don't moan. I like it down there, and you know that Miriam and Gerald go there, and if it's good enough for toffs like them it's good enough for me."

"I might have guessed that you'd mention that tart. Don't you know that madam Miriam has a soft spot for you. She' always sniffing round you. And gormless Gerald's too thick to see the way she smarms all over you."

"But Sylv, it's just a bit of harmless flirting. There's no harm in it. You know it's you I love."

Sylvia knew that moaning at her partner wouldn't do any good. She sighed, "OK, Sorry, but please, at least give the other place a moments thought."

"OK sweetheart, just for you."

He lurched towards here with that familiar look on his face. His body language spoke volumes. She could smell his breath.
"Oh, my God, and that's the other thing. You always stink when you come back from that shithole."
"Oh, but you know that you still love me just as I am." he smiled that smile.
She knew what was going to happen next, and she knew that she wouldn't be able to stop it.
"I suppose you've eaten?" she asked.
"Yeah! There was this new takeaway just up the road, I'm as full as a pelican's beak."
After he had eaten his fill, there was only one thing on his mind.
"Here we go again." she thought. This is where the nightly ritual began, and it was always the same.
"D'you fancy making some babies then?" he grinned.
It wasn't much of a chat up line, but he didn't have anything better in his repertoire.
She succumbed to his charms and then he fell instantly asleep.

It was Saturday evening, another Saturday evening, and Sylv had a very determined look on her face.
"Right Derek," she said, "Tonight were going just around the corner, over that little hill, to MY favourite watering hole."
"But, but, I don't want to, sweetheart. Oh, don't make me go there. Miriam and Gerald won't be there. None of my mates go there, and we'll be strangers."
"Derek, I, am not taking no for an answer. I've made up my mind Derek. Now come on."
She dragged him in the opposite direction to his desires, and he had no choice. Reluctantly he hopped along as instructed.

Sometime later, they returned.
"There that wasn't too bad, was it?" she asked., "And you don't smell as bad as you usually do."
"If you say so, " he answered with an air of resignation, "But that takeaway on the home trail tasted a bit funny. I don't feel very well, I'm going to bed early tonight."
"You mean you don't want to make babies, then?"
"Don't be stupid woman, that's what I was put on this Earth for." he replied grabbing her roughly, and without any sweet words or foreplay taking her roughly and quickly.

Soon they were both asleep.

And that was it! They never woke up. There was no Sunday morning, not another Sunday morning.
Sylvia and Derek were dead, all their babies were dead, and soon Miriam and Derek would also be dead. None of them knew that the previous evening just before they had gone to their respective watering holes chemical warfare had broken out against their species, and they had been viciously and arbitrarily poisoned.

Reporters notes:

The species can only mate after feeding.
The species has legs designed for jumping great distances and mouthparts designed to suck blood.
The species is required to find a source of moisture once every day by paying a visit to the eyes or the anus of the host.
Ctenocephalides canis is an ectoparasite that lives in a wide variety of animal environments including dogs.

## Pretty Red Dress

***This is another of the many incarnations that came about shortly after the death of Gerry Rafferty on 4th January, 2011.***
***He is renowned for writing a wonderful song called Baker Street which features some fantastic saxophone. I mixed his creation and some of the images he painted together with my own personal recollections from Baker Street. The raven haired lass was real, a busker who I met while she was performing in one of the tunnels of the tube station.***
***I used other Baker Street connections like Sherlock Holmes and the Planetarium.***

21st Jan, to 2nd Feb 2011, and 11th August, 2014

There's a raven-haired lass playing blues
on a wild saxophone,
In a pretty red dress and no shoes,
she's a long way from home,
And the swirl and the swoon of a Rafferty tune,
so well known,
Swirls and circles around the walls
of the underground stone.

Somewhere deep in the gloom
of those strange catacombs, a heart beats
She's a long way from home playing wild saxophone,
oh so sweet,
That raven-haired lass, in a pretty red dress,
with bare feet,
Close to where we meet in the evening
at Baker Street.

The super-sleuths look through the pages
in the good book for a clue,
They're chilling out on cocaine,
as she's waiting for another train to come through,
And she begins once again
when the next train pulls into her view,
With the swirl and the swoon

of that well known Rafferty tune.

The grandfather clock chimes
while she's playing her wild saxophone,
That raven-haired lass in a pretty red dress
works wind-blown,
As they dwell on the crimes they don't care
that she's a long way from home,
Nowhere near Baker Street,
and somewhere so cold and alone.

Where wise men can converse
the mysteries of the Universe every day,
So stargazers pretend they understand,
and comprehend, or so they say,
It's so cleverly entertained,
but there's still a nagging pain that's unexplained,
In this overcrowded place we can
all get lost in space, anyway.

Is it all just a dream when no one
hears you scream out of view,
In her man-made black hole she move
body and soul for her dues
She's light years from home
playing wild saxophone just for you,
Close to where we meet
at our Baker Street rendezvous.

If this city's an imposter we find
guilty of selling illusion,
Then both fiction and fantasy
were helping to fuel our confusion,
Just yesterday's heroes
and celebrity zeroes in their fusion,
All our tomorrows in the chamber of horrors
is our one conclusion.

.

If this city's a desert wasteland
and devoid of any truth or any soul,
Well we just have to face the fact
that there ain't nowhere else for us to go,
But after the man and the mystery
have gone we'll still know,
That the music goes on and
will never be forgotten or grow old.

Noodles (Playing with your words)

***Just a bit of nonsense verse with the theme of noodles.***

28th August, 2014

A peculiar crude type of food are noodles,
Invented in China, to be chewed by the frugal,
Four thousand years ago,
Somewhere close to their Great Wall,
Now we just add boiling water,
For instant fast food approval,
But, Never, never, ever twiddle with your noodles,
If you're shrewd you'll conclude that it's rude,
To be lewd with such a longitudinal food.

A weird kind of dog is a labradoodle,
Its neither a Labrador, Nor is it a poodle,
It's a bit of both breeds,
Mixed up like a strudel,
But, Never, never, ever fiddle with a labradoodle,
They'll just wriggle while they piddle ,
on your longitudinal noodles.

And what kind of word is the verb to google?
You've got to agree, That it's highly unusual,
Cause it does just the same thing,
As Ask Jeeves or Bing,
But, It's a riddle if you do all your searching with a google,
When you'll find tarradiddle
in the middle of a doodle.

A quick kiss and cuddle might be called a canoodle,
A little slap and tickle, In a Travelodge in Walsall,
Could lead to your downfall,
If you're fooled into going the full kit and kaboodle,
But,
She may giggle while you wiggle and jiggle in the nude and all,
You really wanted was for her to play a tune on your bugle.

Diversions

***Originally I wrote this story as a stand alone, and I never had it in mind to expand it in any way. Strangely, it eventually became the second instalment of a story that began with a piece called "Obsession" which I had written 6 months earlier. Sometimes I write things in the wrong order. I don't know why.***

15th September, 2014

"God! I hate airports." he muttered to himself as he pulled into the carpark at Stansted. The Ferrari purred to a halt, and Ryan Cousins stepped out, glad that the short trip from Chelmsford through the miserable, continuous drizzle of the September early evening rain was over. He was excited. Simone Taylor, his unbelievably gorgeous Simone, was coming home early.
It had been an unexpected strange text that reached his mobile that afternoon while he was still at work. He had planned to be making an arduous, boring, journey around the M25 to Heathrow the next afternoon in the busiest time of the day. But instead he got a text which said:-
" Hi lovely Sugarman, Flight from Miami rescheduled. Arriving Stansted on American Airlines AMA 3982X landing at 19:30 today. Love you loads. XXX Your loving Monkeychild XXX."

Ryan didn't mind, because his beautiful, supermodel girlfriend would be back in his bed a whole 24 hours earlier than expected. He felt horny just at the thought of what he would do to her, or was it what she would do to him, once they were together in the sack. And, here was a big bonus. Stansted was only 30 minutes easy drive away, and fairly civilised, at least compared to the organised bedlam of Heathrow approached around the intermittent carpark of the M25.
Ryan made his way from the carpark to the arrivals hall, queued up for an Americano black coffee, bought himself an "Evo" car magazine, and settled down within view of the information screen. About 15 minutes later there it was on the screen.
"AMA 3982X landed on time"
He took a deep breath, and his heart skipped 3 beats as he merged into the excited huddle of people waiting for their

arrivers. He knew that he could have waited until the screen said "AMA 3982X in baggage reclaim", but the thought of seeing Simone again overwhelmed him with a delightful impatience. His thoughts focussed on her and only her.
She had been away for 3 long weeks on a modelling assignment in Miami and the Florida Keys. Oh boy! had he missed her. All those nights indoors alone talking to himself, feeling like he'd been abandoned, and then trying to organise going out with the boys to have a few beers and talk football. Well, it just wasn't what he really wanted. He wanted her. He wanted to ogle at her curves, run his hands over her bare skin, and look into her deep green eyes and see that look that told him everything he wanted to know. He wanted to smell her perfume, breathe in the summer meadows in her hair, nibble her ear, tell her sweet nothings. He wanted to wake up with her there, blonde locks spilling onto the pillow, her body gently rising and falling with each soft breath. He wanted that smile when she woke up and saw him laying there adoring her.
Now the waiting was over! There she was! Strutting that confident supermodel strut, pink and purple designer Gucci luggage being carried by a porter. Ryan waved. Simone smiled. They met.
He swung her around in his arms and kissed her passionately. "Wow! you look gorgeous, my darling, I've missed you so much." he said, never letting his gaze move from her eyes. Her perfume didn't smell quite how he had been imagining it moments before, but he thought that 7 or 8 hours cocooned in the air-conditioned prison of a 767 might have something to do with that.
"I've missed you too, Sugarman." she smiled back. He noticed that her voice was different too, but he knew that she always smoked too much when she was away on a modelling assignment. She had told him many times in the past that it might all look glamorous and exciting, but modelling was really hard work. They started the short walk to the carpark holding hands, while the porter followed diligently.
"I'm so tired," she said, "It's been a gruelling 3 weeks. Would you mind, darling, if we skip the travelogue for now? What I need at the moment is to have a nap while you take me home."
He thought that was odd. She was usually bursting with excitement whenever she returned from an assignment, wanting to tell all about every little detail of the exotic places she'd

travelled to, and been photographed in.
He replied, with concern, " OK, If that's what you want, my Monkeychild. We'll be home soon, and then you can relax and tell me all about it."
She smiled a thin smile, and said nothing. Ryan paid the porter and squeezed the posh luggage into the Ferrari, and then opened the passenger door for Simone. She climbed in, reclined the seat, and was in the land of nod before he'd strolled round to the driver's side and started the engine.

There had been no let up in the pattern of autumn drizzle. The Ferrari glided through the evening's early darkness as the couple made their way homeward along the fast and efficient dual carriageway of the A120. He focussed on the road, with the occasional glance to his left, thinking again about how wonderful it would be when he got home with his prize. He imagined them having a long, lazy bath together, drinking Bucks fizz, and chatting about her time away, before going to bed, and renewing their closeness in the most passionate and exciting way.
They turned off the main road near Dunmow, and joined the Chelmsford Road winding down through Barnston. The drizzle turned to an angry squall, and the tall trees at the sides of the country road seemed to sway erratically in the sudden wind which heralded the onset of a thunder storm. The windscreen wipers were working overtime, and it was one of those nights when the normally very effective headlights seemed to have trouble showing the road ahead with any clarity. Ryan eased off the gas. These driving conditions were dangerous, and he wasn't about to take any risks. Slowly but surely they eased their way past the villages of Onslow Green and North End.
The passenger stirred a little in her seat while crosswinds buffeted the Ferrari, but she didn't say anything.

Suddenly the driver could see blue flashing lights ahead, and then a policeman in a high-vis jacket stood in the middle of the road waving the Ferrari down.
"What's the trouble, Officer?" asked Ryan.
"Road's flooded ahead, and there's been a four car pile up near Ford End." the officer replied.
"Bloody awful night. Anybody hurt?"
"Yeah, 3 fatalities, and 2 people in a bad way. Ambulances on

the way."
"Oh that's terrible. At least Broomfield Hospital's not far away."
"Where you headed, Sir?"
"Chelmsford. Writtle, near the green"
"Take the next on the right, down through Pleshey and then follow the road through Chignall St James.
It'll bring you out on the Roxwell Road side of the city."
"OK, thanks, officer."
"Goodnight, Sir. Drive safely."

Ryan turned off towards Ringtail Green. He drove slowly. He didn't know the road at all. The weather worsened. The country lane was more like a stream, and the gaps between the lightning and the thunder were two heartbeats . He seriously thought about turning back and taking refuge in the Butcher's Arms until the storm was over. He looked at Simone, still asleep, and thought, "No. We'll be home soon, if I drive slowly and carefully. She deserves to be looked after. I have to get her home".
There was a sharp bend to the right near Dropshots, and as he turned the wheel there was a flash of lightning, and an ear-splitting crash of thunder like someone had dropped a grenade on the car. Luckily, he had been crawling along, at less than 20 miles an hour. So, he managed to stop in time.
It looked like a crumpled soggy bundle of dark clothing in the middle of the road at first, but the lightning soon showed it was a large man dressed in black with a trilby hat. Ryan put the headlights on full beam, and a few yards from where the man lay motionless he could see ahead there was a dark blue van at right angles blocking the road.
"What do I do now?" he asked himself. Simone hadn't stirred, but his first thoughts were to protect her.
He got out of the car, and was drenched in an instant. His eyes filled with rain, and his smart grey suit suddenly hung like heavy weights on his body. He locked the car, and walked over to the casualty. There was another fork of lightning as he approached and bent down.
"Are you all right, my friend?" he enquired.
The bundle of clothes groaned, rolled over to face him, and looked him straight in his water filled eyes.
He was shocked. It was Colin Johnson an old adversary from the days when he had been setting up his construction business 5

years ago. In an instant the van doors burst open and two men dressed head to toe in black leapt out and grabbed him from behind, roughly forcing his arms down by his sides. The dark bundle eased himself slowly up from the tarmac, and snarled "Hello, Ryan, fancy meeting you here."
In the next lightning flash Ryan saw the reflection of a long steel blade in Colin's right hand. He squealed as the point came rushing in under his ribs on his left side, and then was turned and twisted slowly and agonisingly, as a red warm stream of blood squirted out of his body. He gasped his last breath, and as it abandoned his lungs like a whisper in a distant misty void, he thought he saw her through the rain, smiling. It wasn't that smile that he craved, the Simone smile that told him everything he wanted to know. It was a wicked, malevolent smile.

The next day American Airlines flight number AMA 3983 landed at Heathrow early, at 18:30. Simone didn't understand when Ryan, the love of her life, the only man she had ever loved, wasn't at the airport to meet her.

Westward Ho! Ho! Ho!

***Here we have a bit of a departure from the norm. The story takes the form of a script. It takes a poke at history, the Spanish monarchy, and Christopher Columbus. Perhaps you will find it amusing? At the time that I put this together I had a reason to point out to someone who would hear it at a writer's group, that there's a clear and absolutely indisputable difference between an opinion and a fact. Too many people think that their opinions are facts, and that anything said by anybody else is merely an opinion. What they say is their ultimate truth. What others say can be dismissed as ignorant conjecture."***

19th October, 2014

Westward Ho! Ho! Ho! Is a short play by Bill Tremble-Javelin.

***Scene 1:***
***The court of Queen Isabella and King Ferdinand, (Isabel y Fernando, los Reyes Católicos) in the Alcazar in Cordoba on the banks of the Guadalquivir River one evening in the spring of 1492. Present are the King and Queen and a few trusted confidantes, Carlos Domingo Rodriguez, Ricardo Francisco Garcia, and the King's favourite confidante Pedro Velasquez del Lago de Valladolid.***

King: I hate conducting official business in the evening. Do we have to do this now?

Queen: What do you mean? After you've drunk 2 bottles of our very best Rioja and eaten yourself immovable again?

King: Don't be like that, Queenie. You know I like to be entertained with flamenco on these rainy evenings.

Queen: You've always been a sucker for swirly skirts and maximum derrière, my dear. But we do have royal matters to attend to.

King: Yes, But it's that fucking Ligurian navigator, Cristobal Colon who calls himself Christopher Columbus, the Wop from Genoa again. I thought we dismissed his ludicrous plans to find a route to the Spice Islands by sailing West back about 6 years ago.

Velasquez: If I may concur with your majesty. You are quite correct. Columbus sought an audience with the court after your

majesties glorious marriage in 1469 had united the many kingdoms of the Iberian Peninsula. On 1 May 1486 Columbus presented his plans to our Queen Isabella, who, in turn, referred them to a committee.
Queen: Yes, that was after he had already been to see that disfigured upstart, our sworn enemy, King John II, of Portugal in 1485, and been given the bum's rush because the Genoan dickhead totally underestimated the travelling distance to the Spice Islands.
Velasquez: I remember that he proposed that the king equip three sturdy ships and grant him one year's time to sail out into the Atlantic, search for a western route to the Orient, and return.
**(The King laughed and the Queen tittered, and the confidantes politely echoed their mirth.)**
Rodriguez: Columbus also requested he be made "Great Admiral of the Ocean", appointed governor of any and all lands he discovered, and given one-tenth of all revenue from those lands.
Queen: Typical man, asks for far too much, and gets nothing for his trouble.
King: **(Swigging from a bottle of Tempranillo Rioja, and then giggling like a child)**
Didn't put him off though, did it? No, good old Chris Colon, goes back and tries again. Lived up to his funny name didn't he?
Queen: Why are you so crude after you've had a drink, my dear? If you think he's an arsehole why don't you just come out and say it?
Rodriguez: If I may bring us back to the matter in hand your majesties. In 1488, Columbus appealed to the court of Portugal once again, and that meeting also proved unsuccessful.
Velasquez: I believe he drew a blank because soon after his audience, Bartolomeu Dias returned to Portugal with news of a successful rounding of the southern tip of Africa near the Cape of Good Hope.
Rodriguez: With an eastern sea route to Asia apparently at hand, King John the Portuguese pervert was no longer interested in Columbus's far-fetched project.
King: And ever since then the misguided mariner's been banging on our door trying to persuade us to finance his fantasies. I suppose now that he's living in Cordoba he thinks he can pop round for a Paella Valenciana any time he likes.
Queen: God, I hate paella, can't stand all that seafood with eyes

on my plate.
**There was a pause in the conversation while the King opened another bottle of wine, and poured a huge glass out for each of the confidantes.**
King: Cheers mates. (**They raised their glasses and swallowed hard.)**
Queen: Yeah, Bottoms up King Lush, and you'll have one of your headaches in the morning, el cabezota.

Garcia: So, are your majesties going to see Columbus this evening, or shall I send him on his way? **(Garcia had been silent so far, but was becoming irritated with the lack of focus in the discussion.)**

**The King thought for a while, and everybody else waited for the wheels to turn.**
King: So, we've rejected him before on the advice of our confessors and savants because he grossly underestimated the distance to Asia going westward. Now there is a route east around Africa it all seems a bit pointless.
Velasquez: May I remind your majesty that in order to keep Columbus from taking his ideas elsewhere, and to keep our options open, you gave him an annual allowance of 12,000 maravedis and, in 1489, furnished him with a letter ordering all cities and towns under our domain to provide him with food and lodging at no cost.
Queen: That was probably another great night for our wine suppliers my dear.
King: OK, so let's think about it. The little Wop thinks the World is round, and he can get to Asia sailing westward. So, what are the possibilities?
Velasquez: He's wrong, the World is flat and he falls off the edge and is never seen again.
Rodriguez: He gets shipwrecked in a storm, and is stranded on a desert island.
Velasquez: And is never seen again.
Garcia: The 3 ships he wants are attacked and he is eaten by sea dragons.
Velasquez: And is never seen again.
King: Or, and it is possible, he finds what he's looking for and comes back with lots of spices and other stuff.

Queen: And with a load of gold and silver.
King: Could it be?
Queen: And maybe some decent exotic new food to eat, so I don't have to suffer any more bloody paella.
King: We could just abandon the whole idea and hand the smarmy git over to Uncle Tom.
**All the men laughed.**
Velasquez: Your majesty, the Grand Inquisitor, Tomás de Torquemada, has done a magnificent job cleaning up our glorious nation, and his triumphant work since 1478 in spreading the Spanish Inquisition from Castile throughout the lands is well recognised. We sanctioned his establishment of tribunals in Sevilla, Jaén, Córdoba, Ciudad Real and Saragossa. We could send a messenger to get him here right now.
Rodriguez: Your majesty may find that Tomas is very busy at the moment extraditing Jews from our realm. He has a big project under way after the edict of March 31, the Alhambra Decree.
Garcia: His vicious sidekick Cardinal Francisco Jiménez de Cisneros would relish the job of getting rid of Columbus, he hates all foreigners.
King: Oh Yes, the Red Cardinal. He is a sadistic little bastard. He could do the job, torture old Colon, and then bump him off.
Queen: Before you drunken lot get carried away have you really considered all the options. Think about it. If we give Columbus what he asks for there are only 2 possibilities. He disappears or he comes back. If he disappears; problem solved. If he returns we will have stolen a march on the Portuguese, the French, the Dutch and the English.
King: I wonder what the Pope thinks. We are all good Catholics, and we mustn't upset him.
Velasquez: Well, we do know that some popes have regarded the idea of the World being anything but flat as pure heresy, and set about executing anybody with opposing views, even though Aristotle suggested a spherical realm in the 4th century BC. But I am pretty sure that the current incumbent at the Vatican, Pope Alexander VI, whom we all know as ambidextrous Alex, is very busy converting little boys to Christianity in his own unique way. You could say he has his attention permanently diverted to small things.
**Dirty laughs all round, except for the Queen, who frowned.**

Queen: Get back to the point boys. I'm tired, and it'll soon be time for my bath.
King: OK, what do think we should do Queenie?
Queen: Send him on his way. I don't like him, he looks shifty to me, he has webbed feet, and bad breath.
King: That's settled then. Pedro, do the honours will you?
**Velasquez bows and leaves the room.**
**The Queen goes off for her bath.**
**The King opens a bottle of Muscatel de Valencia.**

***Scene 2:***
***The Alcazar in Cordoba later that same evening. Present are the King, his confidante Pedro Velasquez del Lago de Valladolid, and Cristóbal Colón.***
King: **(In a drunken slur)** Sorry about that Chris old son. It was the little woman who sent you away. You know she's a year older than me, and thinks she always knows everything better. So, you want 3 ships, a year's sailing time, and all that other stuff about "Great Admiral of the Ocean", a big share of the spoils etc. etc. Right?
Columbus: If your majesty so desires and will grant.
King: OK, Chris, consider it done. Put it there my son.
**The King and Columbus do a high five**
King: **(Raising his glass)** Bien Vacaciones and all that bollocks Chris. Pedro here will sort out the detail for you. Oh, and make sure you bring me back some gold and silver, and some tasty foody items for the missus will you?
**Columbus bows and leaves.**
**The King turns to Velasquez.**
King: Am I brilliant or what Pedro? The best king that ever graced the Spanish throne, any throne for that matter. What I say goes. I am so wise, I should never be challenged. Am I not the wisest, most intelligent man that ever lived? Well, tell me the truth Pedro my old mucker, is that not so?
Velasquez: Your majesty is surely aware that I always tell him the truth.
King: No, don't mess about, come on, we're mates aren't we? Give me the bottom line, Pedro. Do I tell it like it is?
Velasquez: With your majesty's permission I would caution you to be circumspect.
King: You'll have to run that past me a bit slower, my friend.

(**Laughing**)
Velasquez: Your majesty, even the wisest and most revered king must understand that in the protocols of discussion we are all separate beings with our own views and fears and aspirations. We must all, whatever our standing in this world, respect the opinions of others, even if we disagree. It is extremely easy to confuse oneself by assuming that everything we utter is an indisputable fact, and not merely just our personal opinion. Conversely, we can also fall into the trap of automatically assuming that everything anyone else utters is merely an opinion to be dismissed especially if we disagree with them. Respect must always be amicably afforded to the views of others whether or not we are in agreement with them. Life is a vast learning curve, and the wisest of men are perennially open to fresh ideas and viewpoints.
King: Hmmm! OK. So, is the World flat or round?
Velasquez: Well, your majesty, we must keep our minds open to both viewpoints. However wise and mighty, and all knowing we are. You must even as the greatest and most revered king be aware that what you say and do is based on your personal view of the world and the people in it. Your opinions are not facts, and you must not react to disagreement with hostility and aggression. Everybody's opinions are equally valid from the highest king to the lowest peasant.
King: You're so right Pedro, what would I do without you, my most trusted confidante?

***Scene 3:***
***The Alcazar Castle in Cordoba 20th March 1493. Present are the King and Queen, and trusted confidantes, Rodriguez, Garcia, Velasquez del Lago de Valladolid, and Christopher Columbus recently returned from his voyage.***
King: How's it going Chris? Got any gold, silver or exotic food?
Columbus: Yes indeed your majesty. We have acquired much treasure for our kind benefactor's greater glory, and many strange new foods.
Queen: Bloody marvellous! What have you got to eat then?
Columbus: Your majesty's treasurer is weighing the gold and silver as we speak, and here are our items from the New World.
King: So you didn't find a way to the Spice Islands by going west then?

Columbus: No, but we found new lands that will bring your royal highnesses much wealth and prominence. I named our first landfall San Salvador.
Queen: What about the food?
**Columbus begins to open several large sacks, and describes each item he has discovered before handing them to the others.**
Columbus: These are brown blobby things are potatoes. You boil and eat them. These leaves are called tobacco. You crush and smoke it. These red pointy things are chillies. They will add fire to your food. These red round things are tomatoes. A sweet fruit. This funny looking noisy bird clucking round my feet is a chicken, a very nice tender white meat. And these small brown pods are crushed to make a delightful confectionery called chocolate.
King: Blimey! Well done Chris. I suppose that you'll want us to finance some more trips then?
Columbus: If your majesty would be so kind.
Queen: Can you sum it all up then quickly Chris, 'cause we're a bit busy thinking about raising an armada to conquer the English right now.
Columbus: OK. This is the bottom line. We had 3 ships, La Santa María, La Niña, and La Pinta. We set off not knowing where we were going. We arrived not knowing where we were. And we returned not knowing where we had been. But all in all it was a highly successful expedition. Perhaps our expedition was based on supposition, ignorance, if not a lack of knowledge, and possibly sheer luck, but it still had enormous validity and significance
King: Yeah! Too right! Thanks Chris. Fancy a glass or 6 of Rioja to celebrate?

**The Spanish royals had secretly hoped that Columbus would be lost at sea and never return. They were delighted with the gold and silver, but confused over the food items he had brought back. Later that night they smoked some potato and chilly cigarettes, and dined on boiled tobacco with chicken cooked in chocolate, followed by a dessert of tomatoes in custard.**

Courgette (The story of Cheryl and Pete)

***How to put together a poem by asking Google to generate a list of vegetables, and then to create a plausible story with a crude but amusing rhyming scheme.***

21st October, 2014

She was a cheeky, curvaceous and charming courgette,
Looking for love on the Internet,
Gorgeous and green,
and obviously willing,
Were her admirable credentials,
And a good sense of humour in her beau,
Were her vegetable essentials.

But the trawl through the trash on the websites for dating,
Just made her despair for that longed-for perfect mating.
She was plagued with no-hopers,
in all shapes and sizes,
A motley crew,
But what can you do with vegetables that don't win prizes?

Cauliflowers from Carlisle, and a sweet potatoes from Peru,
Curly kale from Skelmersdale, and tomatoes, and shoots of bamboo,
Bok choy and choi sum, mustard greens and parsnips,
Artichokes from Jerusalem, and soya beans and turnips,
Lettuces from Latvia, and kohlrabi from Tehran,
A mange tout from Montpelier, an aubergine from the Sudan.

There was broccoli and endives, and radishes and beets,
Brussel sprouts and asparagus, and a few shallots and leeks,
Mustard greens from the Philippines, carrots, celery, and okra,
Onions, spinach, parsnips, garlic, mung beans and alfalfa,
Cucumbers from Chicago,
Peppers and avocados,
Chard, mooli and collard greens,
Watercress and green beans.

A sadness descended upon her,
She began to weep and to howl,
Her search had gone on far too long,
She was just about to throw in the trowel.
And then she found the perfect match, a pumpkin boy from Plaistow,
Her joy was overwhelming when she found her love at last, oh!

They were married in Malibu in a mad whirlwind romance,
And honeymooned in Heaven in a lovely chateau in France,
They set up home in Norfolk, in a semi in Kings Lynn,
And later that year they were proud to be,
The parents of zucchini twins.

The Nutivity 2014 (Oh Little Town of Birminghem)

***The nights had drawn in, the Christmas decorations were up, and the annoying Christmas songs were echoing everywhere in town and on the telly. It was that "Wonderful time of year". So, write something that parodies the birth of Jesus. Put the story in a modern context. Make the characters in the tale all Brummies, and resolve the greatest story ever told with a snappy, happy ending. Introduce a bit of poetry here and there, a bit of fantasy everywhere, and an irreverent attitude. Who cares?***
***This story had various titles over time. It started life with the moniker "The Nutivity 2014 (The fishy tale of what may be a sturgeon birth)". It was subtitled so for reasons I have forgotten. Then it became "The Nutivity 2014 (A gherkin birth)",and then finally "Oh Little Town of Birminghem***

24th November, 2014, amended 27th November, 2014

In the deep mid-winter long, long, long ago,
Two unfortunate souls trudged through the ice and snow,
All the way from Kidderminster to Birminghem
with a cruel wind blowing in their faces, to sign on for a job that paid the government minimum wage on a zero hours contract basis. Fairy Nuff and Pixie Snows were those simple folk. They loved each other, and had recently been married in a same sex gay ceremony by the vicar of Dudley. Pixie had wanted to make an honest woman of Fairy, because she knew that the love of her life wanted a baby, but as everybody knows it's not possible for two librarians to make a baby together. Not by normal means anyway. But surprisingly Fairy had become stagnant, and so Pixie had to ask her, "Who's the daddy?"
Fairy told her the story that a few months before she had a mysterious and exciting vision.
She said," Do you remember that fellow called Ainsley Gaybloke we met on holiday in Caister last year?" Well, he appeared to me in a dream one night and performed a miracle with a turkey baster. And then he told me that I was carrying a very special baby boy for a very important reason. Then he said that the baby boy would be more famous than the Kidderminster Harriers centre forward who had scored 30 goals in the 2001/2002

season. "
"Oh Goodo!" replied Pixie, "I'm so glad that you didn't do the dirty deed with a man. Wow! It's makes me feel sick just thinking about it."

It's a long way from Kidderminster to Birminghem, especially if you have to walk, and have no sense of direction. The two waifs had wandered around for days, going round in hopefully ever decreasing circles, passing through Rowley Regis, Blackheath, Selly Oak, and Edgbaston, before getting very confused. They were so confused that 2 days later they went round again through Rowley Regis, Blackheath, Selly Oak, and Bournville. The wind blew viciously through their thin Primark overcoats, and snow began to settle on the pavements of the bleak winter streets. So there they were, two refugees great with child, wandering the cruel streets of Birminghem cold and hungry, and desperate for work.
"It's beginning to look a lot like Smethwick, everywhere I go." Fairy sang sarcastically as she trudged on.
"Never mind!" said Pixie, "I know we're making some progress, 'cause I saw a sign to Aston back there. So we must be walking in a Villa hinterland."
When at last they arrived exhausted at the Bullring they found to their dismay that there was no room at the Premier Inn. But the bloke behind the reception desk was very kind.
"Yous ladies are from Kidderminster aren't you?" he asked.
They both nodded.
Then he added, "I thought I recognised the accent. Tell you what, there's a bike shed round the back of the inn. Why don't you spend the night in there? "
They were so tired, and Fairy's time was drawing near, so they decided to take him up on his kind offer, even though they had to share their crude accommodation with 3 dickheads from Shepshed. They managed to scrounge £50 from Sir Bob Geldorf, who just happened to be passing by in his Rolls Royce on his way to a celebrity awards evening at the National Extradition Centre. So it was their good fortune that evening when they feasted on a slap up Indian meal at the nearby “Flaming Anus” tandoori restaurant. Then they settled down for a well earned sleep.

It was 3 o'clock in the morning when they were woken abruptly. A bright light shone like a star in the East. But it was only the West Midlands police helicopter with a massive searchlight. The 3 Shepshed Richards saw the bright light shining in the East as they washed their socks by night, and they were sore afraid. Everybody in the area knew that the helicopter cost an absolute bloody fortune to run, and that the local fuzz weren't very likely to fly around in it nonchalantly with any benevolent outlook. No, they had to nick someone otherwise the expense couldn't be justified. There had been a recent case where the fuzz had swooped down and arrested the whole family of Mustapha Shamani because he had committed two major crimes in the same week. First he was late back with his library book, "How to build an I.E.D in your garden shed" and then he had the brass faced Muslim cheek to park on a double yellow line outside the library. It was front-page news when it was revealed that the Shamani family were being detained at the Guantanamo Bay detention camp.

Fairy Nuff wasn't feeling too well. She laid down flat on a kitchen table that had been dumped in the bike shed.

"I think that mutton vindaloo, the 9 onion bhajis and the 5 pints of Kronenburg are laying a bit too heavy on me." she moaned.

Pixie was opening a large jar of cornichons she'd rescued from a skip outside the local Co-op.

"Never mind, love!" she said," Try one of these little gherkins; they're delicious."

Fairy reluctantly nibbled on a cornichon, and to her surprise seconds later she gave birth to her baby boy, whom she had been told by Ainsley Gaybloke to give the name Gee Whiz.

So Gee Whiz was born on a table in a bike shed in Birminghem.

And Yes! It truly was a gherkin birth!

Suddenly all the bikes in the shed rang their bells in homage to the newborn , and the helicopter landed bringing 3 wise men. They were policemen, but they did bring gifts of pepper spray, handcuffs and warrants for everyone's arrest.

Music played in a house nearby as the helicopter took off and the snow continued to fall. It was a well known tune.

"And the boys from Birminghem City blues were singing "We love gays".".

And the sirens were screaming loud on Gee Whiz day.

Now we know the rest of the story, because Gee Whiz grew up to travel the land teaching people by telling them parabolas and one day he became the saviour of all mankind by rising to become the leader of Ukip.

# CHAPTER 7

## Have you seen the Latest Newscast?

***"Well, due to the administration's wonderful medical advances I am now approaching my 179th birthday. I had my Cure All when I was 32 and that is why I look so young today."***

Little Red Riding Hood

***Gary Glitter had just been convicted of crimes of historical sexual abuse. Little Red Riding Hood is a sweet and innocent child. Put the two together in a sordid tale with a shocking ending.***

rewritten for 2015)

Little Red Riding Hood, walks through the woods to deliver food to her sickly gran; she had the order from her mother to stay strictly on the path. A mean wolf wants to eat the girl and the food in the basket, and he secretly stalks her behind trees, bushes, and shrubs. He approaches her and she naïvely tells him where she is going. He suggests that the girl pick some flowers and while she does he goes to the gran's house and gets in by pretending to be the girl. He swallows the gran whole and waits for the girl, disguised as the gran. When the girl arrives she notices that her gran looks very strange. Little Red then says, "What a deep voice you have!" ("The better to greet you with"), "Goodness, what big eyes you have!" ("The better to see you with"), "And what big hands you have!" ("The better to hug/grab you with"), and lastly, "What a big mouth you have" ("The better to eat you with!"), at which point the wolf jumps out of bed, and swallows her up too. Then he falls asleep. A lumberjack comes to the rescue and with his axe cuts open the sleeping wolf. Little Red Riding Hood and her grandmother emerge unharmed. They fill the wolf's body with heavy stones and when he awakens and tries to flee the stones cause him to collapse and die.

"Britney, get down these stairs. Now! This is the third time I've called you."
"But, Mum, I'm busy playing Pet Rescue Saga."
"Brit- ney! For the last time get down here, or I'm warning you, you'll be sorry."
Britney paused the game on her tablet and reluctantly complied with her irate mother's request. At the bottom of the stairs Sandra was red-faced and in no mood for arguments.
"I don't know why you play those stupid Candy Crush games all the time, Britney. You teenagers are all the same; never want to do anything to help. I want you run an errand for me. "

"Oh, do I have to, Mum? I want to talk to my friends on Facebook after I've completed this level."
Sandra put her hands to her hips in exasperation, "Well, you won't be doing that when you get back anyway, my girl. It's about time you knuckled down to your geography homework."
Britney frowned, sighed and sat down on the bottom step; defeated.
"Right!" said Sandra, "Take this leftover pizza to your nan. It's ham and pineapple; her favourite. And while you're there, talk to the old girl. She's lonely and needs a bit of company."
"Why don't you go then?"
"Because I'm sending you, and besides I'm busy with my housework."
"Watching Emmerdale, more like."
"That's enough backchat; just take this pizza and go. Now! Be back in about an hour, Go quickly through the park and keep away from the swings and slides where those awful boys hang around drinking cheap cider and shouting abuse at everybody."
The pizza box changed hands and Britney set off, hangdog, disinterested and muttering underneath her breath, "Parents, Who'd have 'em? Treat me like a kid. I'm a smart 14, not a clumsy 4."
She left the house, strolled to the end of Giro Road and into the Ian Duncan Smith Memorial park, keeping to the path avoiding the bad boys as requested. She found an empty park bench, sat down and began to play Pet Rescue Saga on her mobile phone. After 15 minutes her credit had run out and she had to finish playing. She continued her walk and soon she was outside Grandma's neat little bungalow with rambling roses climbing the porch in Geriatric Avenue. She rang the doorbell which played the American national anthem and waited. There was no reply; so she pressed the bell again and it played "Land of Hope and Glory". Then she went round the back to see if her nan was at home. Peeping through the window she saw no signs of life. "One more try and then I give up." she told herself, and returned to the front door and pressed the bell again. This time it played "Auld Lang Syne". Still no reply. She turned on her heel and went to go home.
As she closed the garden gate a peculiarly dressed old man came out of the bungalow next door.
He had a massive quiff of dyed dark hair and wore a sparkly

onesy unzipped to the waist showing his hairy chest. He was wearing what looked like biker's boots covered in pink glitter.
"Can I help?" he asked.
"I'm looking for me gran," Britney replied.
"It's Tuesday, She goes to bingo on Tuesdays. Last week she won the £500 jackpot, came home very pleased with herself."
"I've got to deliver this leftover pizza, and Mum will be annoyed if I take it back home."
"What flavour is it?"
"Does that matter? It's ham and pineapple if you must know."
"Wow! That's my favourite. Why don't you just eat it? Tell you what! Come in, and I'll make you a cup of tea, and I'll eat it with you."
Mister Gilter's old eyes brightened and as he smiled at Britney she thought to herself, "Why not?"
"Come on then, call me Gary, he said opening the door, "And what's your name?"
"I'm Britney." she replied as the door was shut behind her.
"That's it, girlie. Sit down and I'll put the kettle on. Do you want milk and sugar in your tea?"
"Yes please, but not too strong."
The teenager looked around the room, and sat on a massive l-shaped red couch.
"Ooh! What a big comfy couch you've got." she said.
"All the better to lay down and relax." he replied.
The tea was made and the pizza box was opened. Gary went towards a kitchen draw and came back with a huge sharp knife.
"Ooh! What a massive knife you've got." she said.
"All the better to slice up that delicious looking pizza." he responded.
They began to munch away, and then Britney noticed the music system.
"Ooh! What massive speakers you've got." she said.
"All the better to listen to some good music." he answered. Then he got up and put a CD on.
"Good songs these," he said, "Listen! I think you might like them."
"I'm the leader of the gang, I am" Gary said while looking at Britney, and then he sang with the song, "Do you wanna be in my gang, my gang my gang?"
Britney just smiled, but suddenly she felt a bit uncomfortable at

the way the old man was looking at her. She sipped the tea and nibbled at the cold pizza. After a few minutes the next song started.
"Haven't I seen you somewhere before?" he sang along with the CD, staring at the teenager.
"I don't think so." she replied, as he sat next to her on the couch a little too close for comfort. The music was OK, but she didn't like the way he put his arm over the back of the couch behind her.
"I love you love, you love me too love, I love you love me love" blared out of the speakers and he mouthed the words in her direction. Then there was a track with the chorus, "I didn't know I loved you 'til I saw you rock 'n roll", and Gary asked Britney if she wanted to dance.
"No! But I'll have another cup of tea." she replied as a way of getting him to move away from her.
He went to the kitchen and poured two more cuppas for them. When he returned another song started and he sang along grinning at her, "Hello, Hello, I'm back again!"
He jigged about a bit and then plonked himself down again next to her almost knocking the cup out of her hands. His arm went round the back of her again and then he squeezed her shoulder and turned her head towards him with his other hand. Now he was leering at her, fixing his eyes on hers. She started to feel very uneasy and wanted to get away from him. He was sweating; his hands were clammy, and he was breathing all over her face. Another track started and he sang along again.
"Do you wanna touch me? Do you wanna touch me? Do you wanna touch me? Where? There!"
He grabbed her thigh and began to stroke it. She felt her eyes fill with tears. She was scared, and wanted to run back to her mum.
"I think I'd better be going now," she said timidly, "My mum will be worried about me."
His arm came around her waist and he strengthened his hold on her until she felt it difficult to breathe and said, "Don't go now, We were just beginning to get to know each other a little better."
She pushed his face away and turned her head and then she noticed the knife he had cut the pizza with was still on the coffee table. She managed to loosen an elbow from his grip and with all her might forced it under his chin. His head flew back. In one quick movement she wrestled herself free, jumped up, grabbed

the knife and pointed it at his fat hairy stomach.
"Get your fucking dirty sweaty hands off me! You perverted old git! I'll cut your wedding tackle clean off right where you're sitting." she screamed, and then she threw the cup of tea in his face.He recoiled, and squirmed downwards into the cushions of the couch, covering his face with one hand and his crotch with the other. It was over quickly
She took the opportunity to run for her life, and was out of the door in seconds. At breakneck speed she sped across the park past the drunken bad boys and back to her home. She banged on the door frantically; hoping that the old git had not managed to follow her, but also knowing that he couldn't have run that fast. Her mum opened the door, and Britney burst into tears. She couldn't speak.
Sandra was baffled, "What's wrong, sweetheart?" she asked, "Tell me what's happened."
It was then that she saw the blood stained knife in her daughter's hand.

## Obsession

***I wrote this story as a prequel. Because these pieces were written in the wrong order. this then becomes the first instalment of a story that began with a piece I called "Diversions" which I had written 6 months earlier.***
***I repeat, sometimes I write things in the wrong order.***
***I don't know why.***

4th March, 2015

Colin was limping round the builder's yard on his walking stick when his mobile phone rang.
"We've got problems at the Ingatestone site, Boss. The Polish boys have downed tools again."
"What's up now? Has that arsehole Cousins been stirring them up?"
"I don't know, Boss. Their gangmeister Wazilevski says they're not laying another brick until you pay them what you owe in back wages; says that they've got rent to pay and wives and kids to keep fed and watered."
Eddie was used to mopping up little disputes for the boss. As Colin's right hand man he'd been in the business long enough to know how the men at the coalface worked and thought. But this was different.
Something sinister was going on. Not a week went by without a further niggle on the Ingatestone job, and Eddie was growing tired of having barrow loads of shit thrown at him. Colin had problems of his own. In the past 2 weeks his company had lost a lucrative rolling contract with Wagstaffe's for the buildings maintenance of a large spread of properties owned by a local housing association. This had been the bread and butter contract that kept CJ Builders ticking over, and now it was gone, and it was pretty obvious who had stolen it.
The telephone tension intensified
"I know what's going on," screamed Colin, "I bet you a pound to a pinch of snuff that fucking Ryan fucking Cousins is behind this. He just keeps boiling the broth. I'm going round to see him right now."
"Not a good idea, Boss," Eddie replied calmly, "We need to get the boys back to work quickly. We've got deadlines to meet on

this job, and we're a week behind already. It won't do any good at all to ruffle his feathers. You and I know that sooner or later he will get his comeuppance, and all we need to do is make sure that we're there to pick up the pieces and laugh in his face. One day he'll trip over his size 12 work boots and we will have the opportunity to nick all the work back that he has stolen from us."
There was a pause and a sigh as Colin's short fuse was temporarily snuffed.
"You're right as usual," Colin agreed, "I'll sort out Cousins later. In the meantime what do you think we should do?"
"Well! The Polaks insist on seeing you; so you need to get down here quick, and come with some hard cash, or we'll be up to our armpits in it for certain."
Eddie usually kept the lid on things with a calm approach and he wanted to make sure of an easy outcome, so he added, "Oh! And listen, Boss."
"Yes, mate. What!"
"Take a happy pill on the way here and don't turn up all guns blazing or I'm pretty sure they'll wreck the place and walk away."
"I'm at the yard in Hatfield Peveril right now. Be with you in 20 minutes. OK?"

The chilly April rains always played havoc with Colin's left leg, and as he limped across the yard towards his dark blue van a foreboding cloud hung over him. The extraordinary combination of metal plates, pins and bones holding his leg together enabled him to be mobile, but the downside was the draining discomforting distress in his limited movement which forced him to take painkillers every day. Furthermore, he could never get away from the fact that the underlying cause of this disability had been the impatience of the man he had once known as a true friend and business partner. Ryan Cousins had for a long time ever since the "accident" been the bane of his life.

Wazilevski sat on low wall together with his little gang. They were all drinking strong sweet coffee from a large thermos flask and smoking skinny roll-your-own cigarettes as they chatted quietly in their native Polish. Their faces showed strain and tension, just as the tone of their conversation and their mannerisms illustrated despair and depression. "Waz" was the spokesman; the man who had a competent command of the

English language and looked after the other 3 men. Colin approached him and he stood up and as was customary he shook the gangmeister's hand.
The Boss smiled uneasily, "Good morning gentlemen. What's the problem?"
"Mr Johnson; we have not been paid for 3 weeks. We have no money to pay bills, buy food and get to work. Please! We want to work, but we can't do that for nothing."
Waz smiled. His plea was polite and condescending. Eddie looked at Colin, but both remained silent.
"We are good workers; don't want trouble, but you must pay or we will walk away."
The Boss's fuse was relit and his sidekick saw the blue touch paper about to burst into flames. Colin was absolutely convinced that his arch enemy, Ryan Cousins, was at the bottom of this.
Eddie diverted attention, "OK, Waz, give us a minute would you?" he said with a smile, leading his boss away a few yards.
Quietly he asserted, "There is no way out if you want to have any chance of meeting the deadlines. Pay up or we'll be bollixed. It's the only way, Boss."
Shoulders shrugged in mutual understanding and they stared at each other eye to eye. They both knew that they were trapped.
"OK!" said Colin reluctantly, taking a large wodge of notes out of his inside jacket pocket.
Boss, sidekick and gangmeister stood in a circle and quiet mumbles about amounts of back pay finalised with the passing over of a bundle of cash.
Colin couldn't resist asserting his status as the other Polish boys smiled at their victory by instructing them, "Now get back to work or I'll have you all deported back to your little tin pot third world country."

"We need to talk, mate," the under pressure head man said to his foreman, "Get in the van."
They drove to the Red Lion in Margaretting not saying much to each other. Two pints of bitter weren't going to solve the dilemma, but would serve to loosen tongues a little.
"We can't put up with any more delays on the Ingatestone job. We are already 2 days behind because of the recent bad weather, and if the late completion penalties come into play we'll be working for peanuts. After losing the Wagstaffe contract we

are totally dependent on this job coming in on time, otherwise I have to seriously consider our future options, which might include declaring bankruptcy."
"OK, Boss, I understand. So what do you want me to do?"
"Crack the whip! Keep them bloody foreigners in line; pray we don't have any more rain; and get the job finished on schedule."
"I'll do my best, Boss."
"I know I can depend on you, Eddie, but the situation is becoming all too much for me. My fucking leg hurts so much in this damp weather, the company's in danger of going tits up, and Vivian's operations are costing me a king's ransom."
"How is Vivian at the moment?"
"She's OK; been over in the States for the latest operation, and I've no idea at the moment when she'll be back; soon I hope."
Two more pints were ordered and the subject of conversation shifted.
Eddie quaffed a large bitter fix and looked his boss straight in the eyes.
"Right!" he said, "As far as Ryan Cousins is concerned, I think it's best if we just ignore getting even until the Ingatestone job is done."
"I can't wait to undermine that little shit faced cheat. Every job we tender for we lose to him because he's got the council's planning department wined and dined, the building regulations boys in his pocket, and the local casual workforce running scared if they don't doff their caps to him. We were just lucky to get this job, and now he wants to screw it up for us."
"Yes, I know, Boss. Let's not panic. Like I say, the time will come for us to get even."
The two men finished their drinks, and the van returned to the building site, where Eddie began cracking the whip and praying for fine weather as requested. Colin drove back to the yard and spent the rest of the day going through his contacts book trying to drum up some more work. All he managed to get for his efforts were 3 days work for one man during the following week.
Just before he left the yard a thin brown envelope popped through the letter flap in the porta-cabin. Colin opened it almost knowing what it would say before he read it. It was from Caine and Turner, a local developer.

"Dear Sir,

We are sorry to advise you that on this occasion you have been unsuccessful in bidding for the work to construct a block of 10 apartments on the Chelmer Basin project. We are most grateful for your interest in tendering and hope that we will be able to do business with you in the future.

Yours faithfully

Bernard E. Caine
Developments Director"

"Oh, that just takes the biscuit," the despairing builder angrily told himself, "And don't tell me. I know for sure who got the contract instead of me. It was fucking Ryan fucking Cousins again."
Later that evening he felt very sorry for himself. He never slept very well in the double bed on his own without Vivian to keep him warm. He took 2 paracetamol and washed them down with a large tumbler of Bushmills.

Colin was supervising a delivery of 5 pallets of bricks and 4 of them had been put in position with perfect precision. The skies were dark and angry and icy rain was lashing down. The forklift truck carrying the 5th pallet came towards him with what appeared to be breakneck speed, and he shouted "Stop! Stop!" as he edged backwards noticing that the pile of bricks had become unstable and began to tilt towards him. Then he tumbled full length on his back into some footings still shouting, but the forklift continued on course towards him. He felt each brick hit him like a prize heavyweight boxer was throwing a succession of punches to his body. He screamed as he felt the crunch of bones and 5 of his ribs breaking in slow motion as the bricks toppled over. Ryan Cousins was driving the forklift and laughing as if he were being told a series of one-liner jokes at the Comedy Club as each brick crunched into the helpless builder's body. The slow motion agony continued as the main bulk of the bricks fell in a unified heap on the victim's left leg smashing bones and trapping him underneath.
He shrieked, "It's killing me! It's killing me! It's killing......"
Then he woke up, drenched in sweat, breathless; his heart

pounding like a kettle drum; his arms thrashing from side to side desperately chucking off imaginary bricks. He felt like his ribs had been pounded to brick dust and his left leg was throbbing in excruciating pulses of sheer torture. This was the nightmare that he had endured dozens of times before; the one where Ryan Cousins just sat on the forklift grinning at him with unadulterated pleasure while he suffered death by a thousand bricks.

He knew what would happen now, just as it had so many times before. Now he would lay awake for hours replaying events in his mind just as if he were watching a film on in-demand TV. All of the scenes that led up to the accident would be cruelly laid before him. He would see Ryan and himself being the best of friends, setting up a construction and building business together and having great success in their business and personal lives. They would holiday together with their partners in Balearic and Greek island hotspots like Ibiza and Rhodes. Colin would be with Vivian and Ryan with Simone. Mutual friends would regard the foursome as inseparable. That was the happy bit of the tale.

In this waking nightmare Colin's brain would then illustrate the acrimonious break-up of the company and then reel off every contract the 2 men had competed for. He would see that ever since the accident he had been embroiled in a mutual vendetta against his former colleague Ryan, and how this had become an all pervading obsession. But this time the harrowing thought processes would end differently.

Before exhaustion and the need for comfortable sleep took him away from the vision he found himself saying, "This can't go on. I've had enough. Cousins must die. Cousins must die. Cousins must die."

He fell into a deep sleep with one coherent thought on his mind that stayed with him and would be his first brain reflex of the morning. The situation was no longer merely a competitive vendetta. Now it was an obsession, and Colin was intent on hatching a plan to kill his adversary and take back everything that he considered to be rightfully his property.

He told himself, “Ryan Cousins days are numbered. He is going to be ground into the dirt. I’m going to wipe him clean off the planet.”

The Merryweather

***I'd probably seen a repeat showing of the television series based on Arthur Haley's brilliant book, "Roots", or maybe it was something to do with the 2013 film, "12 Years a Slave" as a reminder of the story of "Roots".***
***Anyway, I did a bit of research and decided to write a long (epic) poem about the triangular trade, and to give it a twist at the end.***

23rd March, 2015

Let me tell you a tale of a ship that set sail
On the cruel Atlantic triangular trade,
From the Liverpool quays,
through the Bay of Biscay,
and down to West Africa way.

The good ship Merryweather was chartered,
With goods for sale or to barter.
With traders or chiefs of the tribes,
Loaded with copper and cloth and trinkets and beads,
and alcohol to make ease with the bribes.

Down to the Gambia or around Senegal
or on the Gold Coast shores,
Trading with guns and ammunition,
The first leg of the triangle was over and done,
So Captain James prepared the ugliest part of the mission.

Slaves were kidnapped, and
Set in chain gangs,
By scouring the lands,
For men and women and children,
Then frog marched to the shores,
To be loaded aboard,
In the most appalling conditions.

Packed in head to toe,
They were herded below,
In their hundreds with no way to move,
Chained to the decks,
With wooden yokes round their necks,
And little food and water to soothe.

Then the Merryweather broke the tide,
For a thirty day ride,
Across the wide Atlantic Ocean,
And in the bowels of ship,
Frightened slaves were all gripped,
By the relentless miserable motion.
In the middle passage of the triangular voyage,
To nothing like a brave New World, and
With the saddest of human treasure,
The men died of dehydration and disease,
While the women were used by the crew,
At Captain James's pleasure.

James wielded the whip with a devilish smile,
For his crew all the while,
That they were sailing on the westward sea,
The natives were danced every now again, and
Was it the bravest or most foolish of those men,
That attempted to break free?

A few slaves succeeded in loosening their bonds, and
Then they jumped terrified overboard,
But every one of them drowned,
'Cause there was no way to be found,
To swim hundreds of miles to the shore.

The good ship Merryweather was bound for Charleston port,
On the fair South Carolina's green fields,
Where the slaves would be quarantined on Sullivan's Island,
Before their fate was sealed.

Traded in the market like cattle,
To live out their lives tending rice or tobacco or sugar cane;
While the ship was washed clean, and
reloaded with rum, molasses and hemp.
Bound eastward to the Liverpool quays again.

Among the slaves standing over 6 feet tall,
Was a proud Mandinka warrior called Ki, and
He watched and he listened, and
Laid plans to escape,
When the Merryweather neared land.

One day's sailing from the Charleston shore,
With the New World in sight and the journey almost done,
Ki broke free from his shackles,
Released two more brave men, and
Crawled up towards the sun.

He opened the hatch, and
Ran over to snatch,
A sword from one of the crew,
But he tripped over a rope,
Fell headlong and broke,
Both of his long legs in two.

He screamed as he fell,
So the crewman just yelled, and
Called for the captain to come,
A slave with two broken legs,
Was worth next to nothing he thought,
So he hung him from the yardarm.

When the Mandinka warrior was quite dead,
All the natives were lead in their ritual dance on the deck,
Where each man could see,
Their brave slave comrade Ki,
Pale, broken there hung by the neck.

To press home his wrath,
The captain finished him off,
By cutting Ki down from the mast, he
laughed as he chopped him to chunks,
With his sword, and threw every piece in the sea.

All the slaves were then whipped,
Into the bowels of the ship, and
Fastened so tight in their jail,
And every man there,
Together trapped in despair,
Began to holler and wail.

Suddenly the skies grew dark, and
Black clouds filled with rain,
A hurricane blew like the wildest beast in the world,
Batten down the hatches,
Make fast for safe haven,
The captain's stern orders were hurled.

The ship spun around, and
Pitched deep and high, and
Rolled from side to side,
For four hours long,
The crew held on,
For the most perilous of rides.

Abandon ship! the captain cried,
When the Merryweather was doomed
Then the battered hulk turned turtle, and
All the crew were hurled into the raging foam.

On that fateful day every man was drowned,
In the treacherous Atlantic seas,
As the Merryweather was wrecked,
But the saddest loss, As the ship was tossed,
Were the slaves still trapped below deck.

Packed in head to toe,
They were stranded below,
In their hundreds with no way to escape,
Chained to the decks,
With wooden yokes round their necks, and
To drown where they lay was their fate

The proud gentlefolk of Charleston,
Honoured the dead,
That washed up later on the Carolina's strand,
But only the few,
That made up the crew,
Were ever buried on America's land.

The slaves all went down with the ship,
Never to be seen or heard of again,
No-one remembers the day in 1815,
December18th in the hurricane rain.

Some fifty years later,
Abraham Lincoln held true,
To steadfast strong beliefs,
In his own words he said,
The citizens of the United States,
Were "half slave and half free".

And the bravest of men,
Would gather and declare,
That could no longer be.
America's civil war,
Had been fought and been won,
To abolish slavery, and
clearly now the time had come,
To give every man "the blessings of liberty".

On the 18th of December, 1865,
The Thirteenth Amendment was declared,
And every slave in the land,
Would hold up his hand,
To remember that day if they dared.

Now when the gales blow ashore,
All the way from the Azores, and
They batter the Carolina strand,
There's a white clap-board church,
Standing high on the hill,
Where the ocean meets the land.

When the wind gets so harsh,
The church starts to sway, and
You can hear the dull thud of an old iron bell,
And on the 18th December of every year,
It summons men up from the swell.

The mists swirl around,
As a pale moon is rising, and
You can hear men holler and wail,
A ghost ship glides silent,
Into Sullivan's Island;
It's the Merryweather in full sail.

Slaves packed head to toe, and
Drowned together below,
In their hundreds with no way to be free
Come dancing in chains round the decks,
Wooden yokes still round their necks,
As the ship pulls into the quay.

Then the slaves come ashore,
Wading in from the sea, and
The column's 200 or more,
They'll crawl up the beach, and
At last they'll have reached,
Safe haven of Carolina's shore.

For 50 years they were trapped,
Beneath the waves worthless and unremembered,
Now they're free from their hell,
Called by the old iron bell,
On every 18th of December.

And at the head of the trail,
Leading the hollers and wails
As the ghostly procession rises from the sea,
It's a proud Mandinka warrior,
Who goes by the name of Ki.

The Guitarist

***This piece is written from personal experience, and depicts a time beginning in my childhood, and carrying through almost to the current date. It is entirely true and factual. Only some of the names have been changed.***

9th April, 2015

Underneath the stairs in a small alcove in the hall the piano laid gathering dust, unloved and un-played, even at Christmas. In the uncarpeted bare floor living room a pre-transistor Regentone radiogram oscillated in and out of a medium wave pre-pirates BBC radio station.
Tommy Steele had been singing the blues for a few years, and then went all comedy on us and told us the story of the little white bull. At about the same time Lonnie Donegan progressed on the same path from singing hang down your head Tom Dooley about a man about to go to the gallows in the morning to asking us, "Does your chewing gum lose its flavour on the bedpost overnight?"
In playgrounds all over England kids enjoyed the kudos of knowing all the words to both of these essentially naff tongue in cheek ditties.
Cliff Richard maintained his respectability when he sang about something called a Livin' Doll long before inflatable women became available. But to be honest we were all still in a dinosaurian age where the song and the singer were king and queen and any instruments employed were poor subjects confined to being just back up devices. A change was in the air.
In the next year the Shadows would twang out Apache, and a one-time session musician called Bert Weedon would come to prominence. Then every kid in the land would want a newfangled electric guitar, buy Bert's instruction book, "Play in Day", and watch his television series of the same name.
My friend John weeks had a Fender Stratocaster electric guitar and a small amplifier for his birthday. I wanted one, but Mum told me that John had a rich American father who worked for Fords. My dad lived somewhere in deepest Romford 5 miles away with a ginger-haired woman called Renee and worked at the chemical factory in Rainham. He only appeared at Christmas, some

birthdays and once a year to take us to Bertram Mill's Circus at Olympia. I never figured out that if John's family were so rich then why did they live in a council house just like ours. Mum was very good at confusing me with convincing arguments.
We weren't exactly a very musical family. The piano in the hall remained unloved and was sold soon after my dad moved out. My German grandfather Maximilian played the violin, my half sister Jutta played the recorder, and my Uncle Friedrich played the accordion. At my oldest half-sister Brigitte's wedding Uncle Fredy provided the music. He was that clever that he was able to play by ear. It was literally you hum it son and I'll play it or whatever the equivalent is in German, Heil Hitler! Impressive!

Not many years later the Beatles and the Stones battled for supremacy over the airwaves emanating from the miniaturised transistor radios arriving from Hong Kong, and Radio Caroline broadcast non-stop pop off the Essex coast replacing the annoying BBC, and swapping any allegiance that all teenagers had to Radio Luxembourg. Still in medium wave, Radio Lux 208 had 2 annoying habits. Transmission faded out and was replaced by something Hawkwind used much later in their album In Search of Space. The square-wave-generator-like interference that interrupted the pop tune eventually gave way again to the 208 broadcast usually just as the song was ending. But hold on, none of the songs ever got to the end, because the Luxembourg boys were only allowed to play the first minute of every tune to circumvent a broadcasting regulation of some kind. And that was the other annoyance.
My first serious girlfriend Denise Frost was a petite and sophisticated, well-groomed 14 years old. She had twin brothers called Michael and Robert, and their mum bought an acoustic guitar and an electric keyboard for their birthday. I was entrusted to look after these 2 instruments for a couple of weeks before the birthday party and dabbled with the guitar, hurting my fingers, making an awful racket, and getting nowhere.
At the birthday party I met an unkempt kindred spirit called Barry Childs and we quickly became friends. Over the next few years we discovered lots of musical things together, like Bob Dylan, Leonard Cohen, Deep Purple, Hawkwind, Led Zeppelin, Roy Harper, and Pink Floyd, to name but a few. Music and concerts and pubs galore were the order of the day. I was deafened by

Deep Purple playing songs from their Deep Purple in Rock album at the Romford Odeon, mesmerised by the virtuosity of Roy Harper at the Cambridge Folk Festival, disappointed with a lacklustre performance by Bob Dylan at the Isle of Wight Festival, and hypnotised by the intimacy of watching all the best folkies in the Universe playing a few feet away from me in the cellar at Les Cousins Folk Club in Greek Street, Soho. Privilege indeed it was to marvel at the playing and singing of Ralph McTell, Sweeney's Men, Pentangle, including the brilliant Bert Jansch, Tom Paxton, and my favourite Roy Harper. Saturday night and Sunday were set in concrete as Les Cousins all night, a few hours sleep on the Circle Line just after 6 in the morning, followed by brunch, and a protest march usually trailing from Trafalgar Square to the American Embassy in Grosvenor Square. Yes! I was a weekend hippie along with thousands of others.
The best thing about Barry apart from the common interest in music was that he had an acoustic guitar, and he knew at least 5 chords. He taught me a little; my fingers hurt, then they bled. I bought books about playing the guitar containing songs that I wanted to learn, and time and again found myself being presented with musical theory on page 5. Bert's "Play in a day" reappeared in my life, and was abandoned very quickly together with at 10 other publications because I wanted to play guitar not learn how to read music. Barry and I both bought nylon string cheapo acoustics to make it easy on our sore left hand fingers. Barry learned a bit of classical, something called Sevillanas, and I strummed my way through the easy 2 chord version of Bob Dylan's song Ramona. The flat, lifeless tone of a nylon string guitar when used for strumming just wasn't good enough for me. So, one Saturday morning when we set off for the Rose-Morris music shop in Shaftesbury Avenue close to Tottenham Court Road tube station, I had my eye on something much better. The Rose-Morris staff were trusting enough to allow anyone to pick up any instrument and have a dabble, and I dared to pick up something rather special. That is where I set my heart on buying my EKO 12-string acoustic guitar, and a week later I'd scrounged the 33 guineas I needed to buy it. It was February 1968, and at last I was equipped to play a proper guitar with excellent tone. The 12-string was a different sound, a fuller, more exciting experience, and instead of single grooves in my left hand fingers

I now developed something akin to railways tracks. Now I had the sound I wanted, the songs came quicker - Blowing in the Wind, Catch the Wind, Desolation Row, She Belongs to Me, and a passable version of Streets of London.
Streets of London was the passport to impressing the girls; the necessary apprenticeship to being recognised as a folkie; the essential repertoire piece of the time, and that was long before it received national acclaim as a Christmas hit in 1974.
Soon, I began to write my own songs, many of which have since vanished into the dustbin of my history. But I also kept lots of lyrics and poems some of which would see the light of day again years later.
What I consider to be my first "worth keeping" song was written in 1973 about my girlfriend at the time. She was a lovely, gentle, dark haired damsel called Annis Harrison, and the song was called "Song to Annis".
The Woodpecker in Hutton Drive was the place to be on any pub night, but especially at weekends. It's now sadly demised as a Tesco Extra, but back in the early 70's I met many a friend there, and most of them played either the guitar, or bass, or keyboards, or drums. There were many very enjoyable jam sessions mostly in very annoyed parent's houses and that was where I mostly learned that jamming with other friends was one the best ways to learn songs and techniques, and to pick up tricks and clever bits.

So, at long last I'd learned a little of how to play the guitar, my fingers didn't hurt any more, and could play using either finger-picking or plectrum flat-picking style. I wasn't a guitarist because I couldn't do those soaring guitar solos that Clapton, Hendrix, Blackmore and Page seemed to make look so easy. The slurring, sliding, swooning, swooping, orgasmic 10 minute virtuoso performance in the middle of a rock anthem didn't fit easily with acoustic 12-strings. I had a try on friend's electrics including Fender Stratocasters and Gibson Les Pauls, but never quite developed the knack. Amongst all the enigmatic guitar heroes one man stood out, and that was John Aldridge. You've never heard of him, but he was by miles the world's foremost guitar player. He lived with his mum and dad in a tiny council flat less than 100 yards from the Woodpecker, wore scruffy clothes, was habitually out of work, had dubious personal hygiene, and chained smoked Old Holborn roll-ups. But he was the best guitarist who ever walked this Earth.

Then life got in the way. Relationships, marriage to Rosemary, offspring, work, career, mortgages, and making ends meet all got interrupted my development, and my best friend became an occasional dalliance with the strings. Most times it just gathered dust in the corner, un-played and unloved just like the old piano. But I still put pen to paper, and wrote poems which would one day become songs. Throughout this doldrums period friends moved on and disappeared from my life, and my brother-in-law Derek took up playing electric guitar and joined a band. Fair play to him that he managed to do what I never achieved and learned to play not only electric, but also lead guitar. No! He can't do those soaring solos that I once craved, but he can play a few licks and single note volleys adequately well. Is he a guitarist? No! I don't think he is, because he learns using something called tablature, which is a bit like painting by numbers. So he is a guitar technician whose playing unfortunately lacks true soul and passion, and he has not one single creative bone is his whole body.

Some twenty years later, when bad health eventually befell me with heart attacks and kidney recurring problems, and I managed to pull my local government pension at the age of 48, I suddenly had loads of time on my hands, and the guitar quickly came back into my life. My technique improved, and I started to assimilate different styles into my playing again. Then I began to learn more about complicated stuff like pentatonic scales and blues scales. That is when all the poems and lyrics I had stored up were eventually given life as I turned them into songs.
By then all my favourite guitar virtuosos were old hat, folk music was on its knees, and just like my brother-in-law the music scene had become soulless and lacking in true passion. There were a few exceptions, but mostly the direction had been determined by music factories like Stock, Aitken and Watermann, and then the non-musical gurus like Simon Cowell and Louie Walsh.
In 1998 I was introduced by my double-glazing fitter to one of my neighbours. That is when a lady called Judy Joslin came into my life and started to instil into me some confidence of my ability to sing and play.

Judy played guitar and sang her own songs, and so did I, so we were kindred spirits for a while.
In !999, after being seriously ill with kidney failure, and being the closest I'd been to meeting my maker, I began to attend the Church of the Holy Spirit, and it wasn't long before the vicar, Nick Hey, found out that I could play the guitar. I'd been there about 6 months when Nick said to me, "We've got a problem with the church band. Can you help please?"
"What's the problem?" I asked.
"Well," said Nick, "Our guitarist, Pete and his family are moving to Somerset in 2 months' time, and we need someone to replace him."
"I don't know if I'm good enough." I replied.
"Give it a try," said Nick, "And we'll talk about it, in a few weeks' time."
I turned up for the practice and jammed along with the band, marvelling at how brilliant Pete was, and when it came to the service on Sunday morning I was so grateful that Pete was a gigantic 6 foot 8 tall and stoutly built because I just hid behind him and mimed most of what the band played. But I grew into the role, and Nick never did discuss it any further, so that by the time Pete left and I couldn't hide anymore, I was pretty comfortable with being the band's guitarist. Thus began an 8 year long on and off association with playing in church bands. There is a difference of course in that playing in church services is not in itself a performance with applause at the end; it's more of a collective celebration with all the glory going to God.
In 2000 I began playing regularly in public at open mike sessions, and then ran the Evelyn Wood Music Club together with Judy for 8 months. I recorded over 70 of my own songs between 2000 and 2008 on demo albums, and collaborated with a few other friends to record about 30 other songs during the same period.
In 2002 and 2003 I passed my exams in musical theory reaching grade 3, but although I have a good understanding I still can't read music. It didn't matter much, because by then we all knew that Bob Dylan, Keith Richard, Eric Clapton and Uncle Tom Cobbley and all could read music either.
Between 2003 and 2008 I also played in my own band called Redberryash, and we were regulars at open mike sessions all over Essex.

Then, at the end of a 4 year relationship with a very beautiful and talented lady in 2008 I was well and truly down in the mouth, and needed to find a new direction. After attending creative writing courses and then subsequent writer's group I enjoyed a revival in my writing of stories, poems and songs, and particularly in my song writing and guitar playing ability. Arthritis in my fingers stopped me playing finger-picking style, but I learned to live with it, and developed my flat picking technique instead.
Now I'm confident enough to play on my own at open mike sessions, and it is my intention here in 2015 to go back to the recording studio and record 24 songs which either myself or friends from the writing groups have provided the lyrics for.
So, am I a guitarist?
The answer is an emphatic no!
I can play the guitar, and I understand what I am doing, and what sounds good. I still can't sight read music, and I don't expect I ever will.
Perhaps I am only an adequate singer, but I think I know how to interpret a song and to put my own slant on it. Some would say that of Bob Dylan. So that's a compliment indeed.
I don't know whether John Weeks ever learned to play the guitar at all, or whether Michael and Robert Frost met a third boy and became Emerson, Lake and Palmer. I've no idea what happened in the lives of my friends Barry Childs and John Aldridge, but it is certain that John never received the recognition he undoubtedly deserved.
No, I'm not a guitarist, but I am a singer/songwriter.

## Lost Child

***Originally this poem was written in January 2006, but I added some fresh elements to the tale, and then it was recorded at Highfield Studios in June 2015 on the CD album "Dangerous Curves".***

8th January, 2006, added to 24th April, 2015

In the pale yellow light of a long seaside evening,
On a nearly empty beach as a fading sunset dies,
Among the salty tasting tang of dampening sea breezes,
There calls an eerie, lonely sound that pulls my urgent gaze.

Under the lazy swoop and swirl of searching seagull glides,
Blurring at the darkened edge of softly lapping waves,
Along a sandy twilight waterline is where I faintly spy,
A lost child, solitary, crying by the sea.

Tears are smothered in the swell,
Cries are muted by the sounds,
She stands up and looks around,
There's no one to be seen; no one to be seen,
No one to be seen.

Where are you my child? My child where are you?
Where are you my child? My child where are you?
Where are you my child? My child where are you?
Where are you my child? My child where are you?

And as the ever moving hand of dark relentless night,
Sweeps away the last few rays of summer's dying light,
A growing mess of deepening shadows swallows up the sound,
And carries her away to be in the warmth of welcome arms.

Tears are smothered in the swell,
Cries are muted by the sounds,
She was lost but now she's found,
On her way back home; on her way back home,
On her way back home.

Bright day is soon abandoned to cool night's persuading charms,
Her failing soft hold now releases, crying ceases, she is safe,
And all remains in stillness are the gently lapping waves,
In worship to the restless spirits of creation and always.

Have you seen the latest newscast?

***The mists of time have obscured where the inspiration came from for this story set well into the future. Who knows whether life will turn out like this later on in our history?***

6th May, 2015

"I was eavesdropping when I heard." said 102J11.
"Really! Where were you?" replied 709A15.
"In the Nutrition Station at Government House 47."
709 laughed.
"Well normally I would tell you not to believe everything you hear, but in this case I'm very happy to tell you it's true."
"You're happy? But it's terrible news, and I'm not sure I'm going to be able to follow the new regulations."
"Listen 102; you are very young and you don't have the benefit of living through the last 2 centuries like I have. I can tell you with great certainty that if the Emperor says it's right then it is."
"But why are you so sure? Doesn't our administration make mistakes?" said 102 with frustration.
709 smiled and began to explain.
"Look!" he said, "Let me go through the history."
"OK, if you must." 102 responded. 709 was very fond of repeating the history. 102 just expected it was what old people did.
"When the Emperor took over we were in a real mess. The world was in financial turmoil, and all our care systems were becoming entropic. We were heading for a global revolution taking us into the abyss. Terrorism, Nationalism, Separatism, arguments over climate change, religious bigotry, increasingly violent food riots were all prominent, and those were only the tip of the iceberg. The Emperor was elected legitimately by the people, and within 10 years enormous strides were made. Not only did he sort out our national status, our place in the world, our absolute global financial superiority, our immigration policy;" he paused, "Need I go on?"
102 knew that when 709 got into his stride there was no stopping him. So he just decided that a reply would be futile.
The elder 709 continued.
"When the administration came up after 12 years with a cure for

all cancers, then all known diseases, and then ultimately a cure for ageing and death itself, how could we not believe in our beloved leader? It goes without saying that having got us out of the European Community his master stroke was to keep the Cure All exclusively for the English people. He'd succeeded only months before in breaking up the UK and devolving our satellite nations; those hangers-on in Scotland, Wales and Northern Ireland. So we didn't have to look after all those whining parasitic spongers anymore. No! Now we were back on our own; masters of our own destiny."
709 stopped and smiled at his companion, giving a look to say "You can speak now."
102 stroked his chin, and thoughtfully offered, "I don't believe that it was just a lucky coincidence that first our great leader kept the Cure All available only in England, and then that global virus of 2029 just killed off everybody else on the planet. I think the administration developed a sort of antidote to the Cure All, and spread it around the planet."
"Don't you see?" said 709 getting more heated, "It really doesn't matter anyway. Who cares about all those Krauts and Dagos, and Wops, and Chinkies, and Yanks, and all the fucking Moslem troublemakers? Did we need to give a shit about whether Scotland had been renamed Nicolandia, and all their stupid claims to our oil? Whether it's coincidence or not, it was just brilliant, because it left us in charge again. Once again Britannia ruled the waves and this time there were no inferior races to upset the apple-cart. It was our world. We were the Gods."
"It wasn't Britannia though was it?"
"OK, I stand corrected. I accept that when we repopulated the rest of that thankfully empty world the Emperor had renamed our nation as Greater Faragia. But didn't he deserve to have it all named after him after all the administration's achievements?"
102 sighed.
"OK, so I accept your version of history as an explanation of how we got where we are today, but I still can't believe that the Emperor is going to reverse the State Programme for Enforcement of Reproduction Management, and that is what I heard sitting here just a few minutes ago."
"My friend, how old are you now?"
"I'm 25 next birthday. Why do you ask?"
"Well, due to the administration's wonderful medical advances I

am now approaching my 179th birthday. I had my Cure All when I was 32 and that is why I look so young today. But because I am ancient in years, unlike you I can remember the old ways before the unfortunately named SPERM policy was brought in. Nowadays, in the year of our Emperor 150, which translates back on my old calendar as 2165 AD, the SPERM policy separates the 2 human impulses of sexual gratification and reproduction of the species into 2 diverse functions. What that does is 2 things. First, it makes it possible to contain population growth by grooming our offspring in a laboratory given the necessary government approval. There's a neat bi-product in that our female citizens no longer have to go through the pain and distress of childbirth, and obviously there are no longer any unwanted pregnancies like in the bad old days. Secondly, all any adult needs to do to acquire a pseudo-orgasm whenever and wherever that is desired, is to take a little pill and wait 10 minutes. Now, I know that all sounds brilliant to you youngsters, but I can tell you that reverting back to the old ways, although it has some risks, is so much more fun."

"I'm not convinced," replied 102, "When we had our relationship counselling back in Educational Training they showed us something horrible called pornography, where people were doing something physical just for pleasure and not for making babies, and it looked very energetic, extremely time-consuming and not to say very messy and unhygienic. To me it looks totally disgusting, all that pushing and shoving, and heavy breathing. I'm not at all sure that I'm going to like having to do it that way when the new law comes in."

"Oh please, trust me 102, you will, you will!"

Recording of CD album "Dangerous Curves" at Highfield Studios

***After a gap of 7 years I returned to a recording studio in June 2015 and laid down these 11 tracks. I played a selection of different guitars instead of sticking to my trusty old friend, the EKO Ranger 12. All the lyrics and music were composed by me, except for 2 tracks.***
***For "I Looked up(Moon Tune)" and "Plant Dying Blues" where the lyrics were provided by a writer's group friend, Estella Boxhall-Hutson.***

1st June 2015

| Key | Capo/Chord | Song Title | Instrument |
|---|---|---|---|
| Emaj | (Open) | Dangerous Curves | EKO 12 |
| Dmaj | (Open) | I Looked up (Moon Tune) | MARTIN 6 |
| Amaj | (2/Gmaj) | Storehouse of Memories | EKO 12 |
| Dmaj | (Open) | I'm Scared (Again) | Starfire BLUE 12 |
| Amin | (Open) | Seasons Resign | EKO 12 |
| Emin | (Open) | Departures | EKO 12 |
| Emaj | (Open) | Plant Dying Blues | MARTIN 6 |
| Gmaj | (Open) | Tricks with Time | EKO 12 |
| Emin | (Open) | Lost Child | EKO 12 |
| Emaj | (Open) | Designer Label Blue | Starfire BLUE 12 |
| F#min | (2/Emin) | Wicked Angels, Luscious Demons | MARTIN 6 |

Promises and Regrets (formerly titled Tricks with time)

***I wrote a piece called "Tricks with Time" back in February 2012, and at that time the poem/song didn't have a chorus. My good friend, Les Melleney suggested that I might need one. So I wrote the "Sometimes I wish I'd stopped ...." addition as a chorus, and changed the name of the piece to "Promises and Regrets". I also converted from the third to the first person. Sometime later I had the privilege of performing the song at the Cramphorn Theatre in Chelmsford.***

21st December,2011 to 8th February, 2012
(Chorus added 5th June, 2015)

Well, I was naked on arrival, with nothing to bring,
But hell-bent on survival, with new songs to sing,
Growing into someone with hopes, and plans, and dreams,
When I was so very young and the world was my pearl,
With my heart on my sleeve; my mind in a swirl,
Impatient and impetuous, but time was not what it seemed.

Now most of my experience is in the rear view mirror,
Reflections and memories as my hair grows grey and thinner.
Now wonder's turned to wisdom and emptiness into space.
Can I content myself with how I spent my days?,
Did I grow happy with my lot or just set in my ways?,
As time became etched in every precious line of my face.

Sometimes I wish I'd stopped to take a longer look
at some of the good times along your way.
As years and years went rushing by so fast before my eyes -
And the promise of tomorrow turned
into the regrets of yesterday.

Did I do it all for love; did I do it for art?,
Did I lead with my head or follow my heart?,
Can I put it all down to providence or fate?,
Will I fall as a saint or stand tall as a sinner?,
Can I live long as a loser or die young as a winner?,
Am I a fool rushing in or an angel who hesitates?

Sometimes I wish I'd stopped to take a longer look
at some of the good times along your way.
As years and years went rushing by so fast before my eyes -
And the promise of tomorrow turned
into the regrets of yesterday.

I remember when my life was still way ahead in view,
And I had so many things to look forward to,
And I held no fear for the mountains I needed to climb,
Then all my days and years went flashing by,
And some of those I love had to say goodbye,
Then I found my mind was playing tricks with time.

## Henry's Operation

***Henry Collins was a member of the White Horse Writer's Group ,and told the members at a meeting in June 2015 that he was due to go to hospital for a delicate operation. This provided an opportunity that was difficult to resist. I wrote this humorous poem to mark the occasion, and celebrate the successful outcome.***

13th July, 2015

I'm going to tell you a story of a man called Henry;
He's in his 80's you know,
He joined our gang at the White Horse Group about a year ago.
We found out he was Jewish, and Sylvia is his wife,
but we don't get tales of bar mitzvahs and bagels in his life.
No, Henry sailed the seven seas in his merchant navy days,
but Neptune and Poseidon are not in his watery escapades.
And then he ran a business with second hand cars to be sold,
Where all his deals were kosher, and all his wheels were gold.

When Henry tells his stories we find some common themes,
Tank commanders in the war, the courage of the Ghurkhas,
Vikings rebelling against poetry, grand Kings and Berserkers,
And he's in love with Joanna Lumley
and the charitable things she's done,
Even at his advanced years he'd probably like to give her one.

Poor old Henry's got a problem, and it's not easy to talk about,
So he went to see the quack to sort his problem out.
Doctor Quack went on the attack and then threw his hands in the air,
He said that there's no way my friend I'm going to look in there.
I'll send you to see a specialist; someone who's in the know,
A potholing man from Nottingham who'll go where I won't go.
You see Henry's predicament was delicate,
and he'd deliberated for some time,
Whether he should try to get help from a guy
who goes where the sun don't shine.

The day of destiny arrived and Henry nearly ran away in fright,
The potholing man from Nottingham donned his overalls
and a helmet with a bright light,
He took a telescope and a camera probe,
a cheese and chutney sandwich and a thermos flask,
He was well prepared for his expedition
'cause he didn't know how long it would last.
After clambering around for quite some time
the expedition returned to base station;
That's when the potholing man from Nottingham
told Henry he'd need an operation.
Then quickly he rushed off, waving good luck and mazal tov.

On the 6th of July, Henry waved goodbye
to Sylvia and went to meet his doom,
He twiddled his thumbs and thought of Joanna Lumley
as he sat in the waiting room.
Then, later he lay in his hospital bed just prior to his operation,
As an 8 strong team of doctors and students
gathered round for his pre-op explanation.

The team leader introduced everyone by name,
and they all smiled at Henry polite and inane,
Then they gathered in closer by Henry's bed,
to hear the words of wisdom that were being said.

Now, said the anaesthetic man
with a gas bottle and a face mask in his hand,
I'm going to put you into a long and comfortable deep sleep,
It's my job to make sure you don't wake up before
the surgeon's had a good peep,
At what's ailing you down below where Doctor Quack feared to go,
But where the potholing man from Nottingham
told us something that we needed to know.

Well, said the surgeon man
with a selection of scalpels in his hand,
it's important my dear Henry that you understand,
We are going into the unknown here,
and we don't know what we'll find,

But we're going to do our best to put your mind and rest,
so I'll lay it on the line.
It's possible that we may have to cut bits of you away
and take them for examination,
But if this comes to pass, we'll do skin grafts up your arse,
so there'll be no need for too much consternation.
However, I must warn you
that there may be a small problem
you'll experience if we have bad luck,
But I've done this job before many times with great success
and I'm not a meshuga or a schmuck.
Sadly it's not a curable situation but I seriously doubt
that you will come to any harm,
You see, if we do have to make grafts we'll be taking the skin
from the lower part of your forearm.

At this point in the consultation the 8 strong team
all sniggered and tried very hard to hide their grins.
Henry was baffled with what they were amused by
and in no mood to be taken in.
He asked, what's so funny as the team leader checked his watch
indicating it was really time to go,
And the surgeon looked Henry straight in his eyes and said;
I'm sorry to have to tell you that it is possible post-op
that you won't know your arse from your elbow.

Empty Chairs

***Empty Chairs was a homework subject matter, and this was my contribution. It was always written as a song. There is a very consistent structure to the words and phrasing. The song was recorded at Highfield Studios on the CD album" And the band Played On" in November 2015. I also had the privilege of performing the song at the Cramphorn Theatre in Chelmsford.***

10th September, 2015

Empty rooms can whisper secret, hidden stories;
they can tell histories, of tragedy and glory,
But, they make me wonder where all the happy people went;
could it be they're futures were never heaven sent,
while they were whispering
in empty rooms? Empty rooms, empty rooms whisper truth.

Empty places; sometimes make you feel so small;
where time stands still before you know you're heading for a fall,
But, they make me wonder where all the happy people play;
Have they all gone to horizons far too far away,
while they were waiting
in empty places? Empty places, empty places can't tell lies.

Empty hearts may be longing to be filled with joy and love;
seeking out perfection, wanting to be hand in glove,
But, they make me wonder why would your heart want to go on,
broken and beyond repair, when the one you love is gone;
while you're still longing?
Empty hearts, empty hearts, empty hearts that will not mend.

Empty chairs, sitting there, vacant places fill the space;
missing persons, all forgotten, disappeared without a trace,
But, they make me wonder if my heart would want to be,
in empty rooms, solitary, in empty places, only me,
lonely in the cruel despair.
Empty chairs, Empty chairs, empty chairs just sitting there.

Raven Haired Lass - Return to Baker Street

***This is another of the many incarnations that came about following the death of Gerry Rafferty on 4th January, 2011. Again I used Baker Street connections like Sherlock Holmes and the Planetarium, and then my own personal recollection of the raven haired lass who was a busker performing in one of the tunnels of the Baker Street tube station.***

21st Jan, to 2nd Feb 2011 and 2nd/5th October, 2015

If the sounds of a busker might spill out to the light
will the hounds of the Baskervilles howl in the night?
Sherlock Holmes and Doctor Watson may debate with delight
neat crimes and sweet passion at a house of high fashion.
And a raven haired lass plays the blues in a pretty red dress and
no shoes close to 221b Baker Street.

Was it all just a dream or a subconscious stream
of images blurred and obscure?
But it all seemed so real somehow
and the way that I feel right now
I'm sure that I know what I heard.
Yes! I'm sure that I know what I heard

Can wise men lift the curse from the mysteries of their universe
and stargazers pretend they understand and comprehend?
Look! Just a few yards away they queue in the rain to pay
to view historical false faces standing silent in their places,
And a raven haired lass plays the blues
in a pretty red dress and no shoes, down in Baker Street.

Was it all just a dream or a subconscious stream
of images strange or absurd?
But it all seemed so real somehow
and the way that I feel right now
I'm sure that I know what I heard.
Yes! I'm sure that I know what I heard

She's a long way from home playing her wild saxophone;
Yes! that raven haired lass in a pretty red dress.
And the swoop and the swoon of well-known Rafferty tune
swirls and circles around in the spaces underground,
in the strange concrete catacombs
somewhere deep in the dimly lit gloom, down in Baker Street.

Was it all just a dream or a subconscious stream
of images obscure and blurred?
But it all seemed so real somehow
and the way that I feel right now
I'm sure that I know what I heard.
Yes! I'm sure that I know what I heard.

The Swirl and the Swoon - Baker Street revisited

***Yet another of the many variations on a theme that came about following the death of Gerry Rafferty.***
***The raven haired lass performing in the Baker Street tube station leads into Sherlock Holmes and the Planetarium, and in this variation Madam Tussauds is mentioned."***

A distillation from Pretty Red Dress, 4th/6th October, 2015

Rebecca was a long way from home;
a raven-haired lass, in a pretty red dress,
blowing wild on a blue saxophone.
When the next train pulls into her view
she begins once again with the swirl and the swoon
of that Rafferty tune.

The super sleuths looked
through the clues in the good book;
they're fuelling and cooling their brains
chilling out on cocaine,
a tick-tock grandfather clock measures time out again,
and then loudly chimes while they dwell
on the crimes.

In a crowded cosmic place we can all get lost in space.
It's so cleverly explained, so we're amused and entertained.
but at the heart of the game there's still a nagging pain.
Is it all just a dream when no one
hears you scream?

Where yesterday's heroes stand beside celebrity zeroes
there's a place for all our tomorrows in the chamber of horrors,
Are we tried and found guilty of selling illusion,
while both fiction and fantasy help feed
the confusion.

But we know this city's a desert
and devoid of any truth or any soul,
and if we try to face the facts
there ain't nowhere else for us to go.

But after the man and the mystery have gone we still know that the music goes on, and will never be forgotten or grow old.

## The Man in Dark Glasses

***Have you ever met a trendy vicar? I have, and this poem is about him.***

22nd October, 2015

The man in dark glasses was a man of strong principles.
(He spoke in a high voice because he'd broken his testicles)
He strides around so self-assured, confident, and invincible.
It's a mystery what lies behind his determined expression,
but it is clear what we have here is a man on a mission.

Hush puppies, Ben Sherman shirt, dirty finger nails,
and a goatee beard;
this man he stands out from the crowd
but he doesn't look strange or weird.
He oozes no charismatic charm
but there's something proud and strong
as he steps in quickly through the door
and sweeps softly through the throng.

Could it be that he's a Jihadi terrorist
or an urbane urban guerrilla,
a rambling gambling man
or an undercover mercenary killer?
Do we fear him or revere him
or think that he's a threat?
Does he work for Wonga or 118,
and has he come to collect a debt?

He doesn't need a posh Armani suit
and a vest that's bullet proof,
He can answer every difficult question
because he knows the truth.
He's not with the Russian Mafia
the Cosa Nostra or the mob,
He targets people like you and me,
'cause recruiting is his job

He gets his instructions from heaven,
a source that's high above;
the only bullets that he fires
are salvation, peace and love.
There's a New Testament in his pocket
and round his neck a cross;
he's hell-bent on a good cause
and the Lord Jesus is his boss.

He'll put an arm over your shoulder
and comfort you in distress;
smile and say "It'll be OK",
and pray to put your mind at rest.
I suppose the bad breath, the moped
and the crucifix were a clue,
'cause he's a hitman for Jesus
and he's looking for you.

Recording of the CD album "And the Band Played on" at Highfield Studios

***Only 5 months after my return to a recording studio with the CD album "Dangerous Curves", I went to the Highfield Studios again to record "And the Band Played On".***
***In November 2015 I laid down these 11 tracks.***
***Once again, I played a selection of different guitars.***
***All the lyrics and music were composed by me, except on two tracks, "Where did all the Giving Go?", by Linda Dyer, and "Where the River Bends", by Margaret King.***

November 2015

| Key | Capo/Chord | Song Title | Instrument |
|---|---|---|---|
| Emin | (Open) | And the Band Played on | EKO1 |
| Abmaj | (3/Gmaj) | Stirring Words | MARTIN 6 |
| Dmaj | (Open) | Where did all the Giving Go? | EKO12 |
| Gmaj | (2/Gmaj) | Where the River Bends | MARTIN 6 |
| Amaj | (2/Gmaj) | Clock of the Seasons | EKO12 |
| Dmaj | (Open) | Muddy Waters | Starfire BLUE 12 |
| Gmaj | (Open) | An Englishman Abroad | EKO12 |
| Cmaj | (Open/ | Please(Ribbons of Reason) | MARTIN 6 |
| Gmaj | (Open) | Hideaway | EKO12 |
| Gmaj | (2/Open) | Empty Chairs | MARTIN 6 |
| Gmaj | (Open) | Last Song for You | EKO12 |

## Railroad Man Blues

***This came out of the blue, probably at a time when I was listening to far too many songs about travelling on trains. There are, as you might expect a number of naughty metaphors illustrating the railroad man's intentions and relating to his train driving prowess.***

17th November, 2015

I'm a railroad man and I'm waiting at the junction
for the signal to change.
I've got 50 dollars in my hand
and I'm thinking 'bout a woman all dressed in red.
Gonna lay my hammer down.
and let you blow my whistle, babe.
Blow my whistle, blow my whistle 'til I lose my tune.

Now I'm a runaway train,
steaming down the mountain on a cannonball run.
I've got a mighty head of steam
and when I get into town I'm gonna have me some fun.
Gonna lay my hammer down.
and let you blow my whistle, babe.
Blow my whistle, blow my whistle 'til I lose my tune.

Been away too long
missing my home comforts and bed that's soft and warm.
Now I'm homeward bound
with a powerful engine and a rhythm so strong.
Gonna lay my hammer down.
and let you blow my whistle, babe.
Blow my whistle, blow my whistle 'til I lose my tune.

Auction (If Things Don't Change)

***A true story about what was happening at an ancient Inn in Maldon. This prompted me to write a poem about how the destruction of our history and it's artefacts is a criminal injustice.***

17th - 22nd November, 2015

***Essex Chronicle, August 27, 2015***

***Hotelier Reassures He Has Not Closed Up;***
***Concerns as Blue Boar Hotel is boarded for 'Refurbishment Work'***

***A WELL-KNOWN hotelier has allayed fears***
***that he plans to close Maldon's famous Blue Boar Hotel.***

***Concerned residents had noted that the grade two listed***
***building had been boarded up over the past week,***
***sparking worries that it had been set to close down***
***after a recent dispute between owner John Wilsdon***
***and Maldon District Council's planning team.***

***Fined At the start of this month, Mr Wilsdon was fined***
***in excess of Pounds 5,000 by Chelmsford Magistrates' Court***
***over a planning breach at another of his Maldon sites,***
***The Sunny Sailor pub.***
***He told the Chronicle the current state of the Boar Blue***
***wasn't linked. The 65-year-old from Coach Lane said,***
***"Maldon is a town of bloody losers who have nothing***
***better to do than make up stories,"***

Tall harvest has been taken in;
low stubble has been burned,
stark fields are brown and bare now
and Autumn leaves have turned.
Vast gathering flocks are heading South
in search of gentle sun;
dark heavy skies load up with chills
now Winter's time has come.
If things don't change they'll stay the same;*

will history be to blame?*
Under the hammer we must go; going, going gone**.

Somewhere way down in Maldon Town
is a place on Silver Street
with a fine Georgian facade.
There's a 14th century oak-beamed inn
and a cobbled black courtyard.
In bygone days stage coaches swayed
in warm Summer and cold Winter,
and on the way changed horses here
between Aldgate and Southminster.
If things don't change they'll stay the same;*
will history take the blame?
Under the hammer we must go; going, going gone.**

Six hundred years of history
should be safe behind these doors.
Kings and queens may have been seen
to walk these hallowed floors.
So can we airbrush history and discard its legacy
like a broken tree that's fallen?
Place character and its relics
under the hammer and sell them off for auction?
If things don't change they'll stay the same;*
and who will take the blame?
Under the hammer we must go; going, going gone.**

Is the Blue Boar to be stripped bare
and pillaged; its ambiance no more,
its character and charm hung, drawn and quartered
before its shown the door?
Will the shiny black cobbles of the courtyard weep
and be finely glazed with frost
as if to display the cold heartless way
that no one counted the cost?
If things don't change they'll stay the same;*
Sometimes it's clear where lies the blame!
Under the hammer we must go; going, going gone.**.

Next on Britain's Got Talent
Jesus Christ will be crucified again
for entertainment on Saturday night.
The greatest show on Earth is on
and Simon Cowell's bought the broadcasting rights.
Pretty soon they'll demolish the Pyramids
and sell them off for hard-core,
before they dismantle the Eiffel Tower
to put iron railings along the shore.
If things don't change they'll stay the same;*
will history take the blame?
Under the hammer we must go; going, going gone.**

Is Maldon really a town of bloody losers
who have nothing better to do than make up stories?
Perhaps the man behind the plan
is determined to destroy the Blue Boar Inn?
There are hidden truths in every move
that sacrifices value on the altar of financial gain;
secrets and lies, pleasure and pain,
laughter and sighs, sunshine and rain.
If things don't change they'll stay the same;*
Sometimes it's clear where lies the blame!
Under the hammer we must go; going, going gone.**

So here we are once again in Winter coats
and at the bus stop wait
to wonder how the world will change
as we stand at New Year's gate.
Whatever the future has in store
you can be sure of one thing.
Our world is filled with those who know
the price of everything and the value of nothing.***
So when things don't change they'll stay the same;*
in this one case we know who's to blame.

**Author Unknown*

***Adapted from KNEES UP MOTHER BROWN a traditional party song:-*

*"Knees up Mother Brown, knees up Mother Brown*
*Under the table you must go, Ee-aye, Ee-aye, Ee-aye-oh*
*If I catch you bending I'll saw your legs right off*
*Knees up, knees up never get the breeze up*
*Knees up Mother Brown"*

**** Oscar Wilde said:-*
*'A cynic is a man who knows the price of everything, and the value of nothing.'*

## Something Quick for Christmas

***It was getting near Christmas and I had to write something to appease the writers group.***

8th December, 2015

Recently,
a very powerful man in a position of authority
confidently advised me with absolute sincerity
that pretty soon we'd see an end to the blight we call austerity.
Was that something quick for Christmas?
I don't know!

And then,
he was quick to add that he was closing all the food banks
to improve the distribution of ministerial finance
and pay for the war in Syria
by building lots of planes and tanks.
Was that something quick for Christmas?
Certainly not!

Later,
our glorious world leaders gathered
in a palace in Mumbai.
Angel Merkel told them all to jump
and David Cameron said, "How high?"
and then she kissed him on the cheek
and waved us all goodbye.
Was that something quick for Christmas?
I very much doubt it!!

Dear oh Dear!
Heaven forbid that the Americans
should control the war against our new foe.
Some call them ISIS, or ISIL or Daish
and some still don't know.
It won't be long before the Yanks
bomb IKEA, Argos, ALDI and Tesco.
Was that something quick for Christmas?
I don't know!

There's something wrong with Christmas
and it leaves me extremely vexed;
it's about all those peculiar people
who spell Christmas with an "X".
Xmas it is not, Christmas it most definitely is,
take Christ out of Christmas
and all you've got left is
Business
Was that something quick for Christmas?
Yes it was!

# CHAPTER 8

## Isn't this Exciting

***"Isn't this exciting? And you're all invited to come along and listen to the band. They'll take it to the max with unprotected sax syncopating with the piano man."***

Time for a change

***It's the end of another long Winter and that certainly makes it time for a change. We are all prisoners of time. Many lives are based around commuting every weekday, after waking in the working day mornings to an alarm. In the Winter that sometimes seems to be all there is. So here comes the Summer, and wouldn't it be good to enjoy some freedom? The sort of freedom you might get by drifting nonchalantly along a shoreline in a little boat, warmed by the sun, andf cooled by the breeze, and carefree.***

Written 23rd March, 2016

Grandfather clock chimes out of tune,
in a dusty corner of a musty room.
Old; out of time, bold, out of tune.
Nobody cares 'cause nobody's there.

Station clock hangs high and precise,
clicks chop the air and grip like a vice.
Loud, the moment hangs, proud it harangues,
the platform crowd; insistent, clear and persistent.
Go home, go away, come back tomorrow,
or another day.

Alarm clock clangs a surly warning;
once again, again it's early morning.
Rise and shine, raise your head,
go to earn your daily bread.
Jump aboard the money go round,
selling your brain on the gravy train.

Oh, let me be once again on a small red boat,
with large white sail, free and afloat,
no clocks, no time; just the sea and the sky, and me,
alone on the breeze, in a calm summer haze,
not counting the hours, or counting the days;
at peace,
un-tamed,
by the cursed chains of time.

Landscape

***"Perhaps these are real questions about why the human race persists with tribal war and conflict. Wars and the battles fought take place on a landscape. Think of the devastation wreaked across Northern France and Belgium in the First World War.***
***Then there's destruction on an unimaginable scale across the whole of Europe from the Atlantic to the Urals ,during the Second World War.***
***IIt still goes on today all around the world.***
***The haves and the have nots fight it out, and destroy what they were fighting for in the first place. Not only the people are victims, but also the landscape.***

Written 4th April, 2016

All too often trembling hands of fate's capricious whim
have clenched in stubborn rage to fuel the coming storms,
warriors riding roughshod across the plains of dark history,
with the menace of a tainted wounded beast,
to curse all quiet men of peace
and stir cruel men of war to arms.

Under shadows deep and long, banners aloft with evil schemes,
spilling from the iron gates of tyranny and bloodlust,
legions of sordid hell-bent soldiers of misguided fortune
invade and scavenge my landscape with bigotry and false religion,
intent to undermine all of
what is good and true and fair.

Have we learned no lessons from Waterloo to Vietnam,
from Auschwitz to Afghanistan, from Stalin to Saddam Hussein,
from Hiroshima and back again
for peace and quiet and no more war?
And when millions of bloodstained refugees
are banging on my door
Will I wonder once again
what in Heaven's name is all this fighting for?

Because among desolation Spring still comes
and flowers tall and proud still grow
and my landscape moves in cycles
from green grass to pure white snow
and back again as our tiny fragile weary World
round and round keeps turning.
So must it be that through all my many years
from cradle to the grave
the rampant raging fires of hate will be forever burning?

## Inspiration, perspiration and constipation

***Every now and again I like to pin a lot of different subjects together to create a form of poetry that illustrates a connection. This an example. I think maybe it just about works?.***

Written 1st May, 2016

I never intended to insult your intelligence
with innuendo and pride,
by taking three words like inspiration,
perspiration and constipation,
and placing them side by side, to imply
that I knew more new words than you,
or you could guess less of the best words than me,
you see?.

Inspiration never stays;
a fleeting glance and then it strays, away.
When no inspiration comes,
must I sit and twiddle my thumbs,
or pick at tiny literature crumbs,
finding word energy come what may?

Perspiration's never fun,
Sweating or glowing in the sun, unsure.
When far too much perspiration flows
from open pores that will not close,
should I just sniff and blow my nose.
waiting on a remedy to cure?

Constipation isn't nice,
when stomach cramps grip like a vice.
When constipation strikes my brain
and leaves my system heavy in pain.
should I sit and squit and strain
trying to relieve me at any price.

In never intimated I'm incapable of intensity
and insinuation in rhyme,
by taking three words like inspiration,
perspiration and constipation,
and placing them one after another, in line,
so that I can become oblivious to
the obscure and the obvious,
and sensitive to common-sense just one more time.

Some say that art is ten percent inspiration,
and ninety percent perspiration,
and they never mention constipation at all.
What of it?
It's OK if you're uninspired,
be content to just sit and perspire,
'Cause you know they're all full of shit.

Isn't this exciting?
(A glorious tale of unprotected sax)

***For several years I had been attending lunchtime concerts at the Cramphorn Theatre in Chelmsford. These were one hour musical performances in many genres from classical, through jazz, to folk music, and lots more.***
***The host was a wonderful fellow called Jeffery Wilson, a virtuoso saxophone blower.***
***Jeffery had a catchphrase which he uttered frequently, and always with a smile, "Isn't this Exciting?"***
***One afternoon after attending one of Jeffery's excellent jazz sessions, I decided to try and write a song using this phrase, and perhaps a jazzy musical tone.***
***I'd never done that before.***
***After I'd had the opportunity to play the song for Jeffrey he asked if I was willing to perform the song on stage for one of the lunchtime concerts featuring new musical works.***
***It didn't take much persuasion."***

Written 28th February, 2016 and 18th April, 2016
and 28th April, 2016 and 2nd May, 2016

I like a little theatre, and it don't get much better
than early on a Wednesday afternoon.
So I'll be pleased to invite you
to something I'm sure will delight you.
Tell me isn't this exciting? Oh Yeah!

Jazz men there will play the tunes to please
Exchanging blows and tickling ivories.
When the tune is done someone asks you just for fun
Isn't this exciting? Oh Yeah!

Piano man's a ragtime blues machine
alto sax tries a new routine
playing Russian roulette in a clarinet duet.
Isn't this exciting? Oh Yeah!

Isn't this exciting? And you're all invited
to come along and listen to the band.
They'll take it to the max with unprotected sax
syncopating with the piano man.

In this little theatre, well it don't get much better
than early on a Wednesday afternoon.
So accept your invitation
to join the Wednesday celebration
Tell me isn't this exciting? Oh Yeah!

Listen to that smoking razzamatazz
in E-flat and B-flat and singing scat.
You can fill your bag
with Wednesday afternoon jazz.
Isn't this exciting? Oh Yeah!

Isn't this exciting? Oh Yeah!
Isn't this exciting? Oh Yeah!
Isn't this exciting? Oh Yeah!

Abandoned again

***Feeling lonely and this came out of a quick pen.***

19th May, 2016

A rain storm of emptiness fills my tomorrows
A chill wind of sorrow blows through my bones,
A snowdrift of heartache falls heavy on my dreams
Abandoned again, and left all alone.

You made me promises you just couldn't keep
True love's just a myth and your kisses were cheap
Your eyes told a story, an unfaithful deceiver
I lost faith in your truth and became unbeliever.

## Don't Talk to Me about Gherkins

***One of my writer's group colleagues, Estella, has a very good friend and neighbour called Ernie, whom we have all met on several occasions when he picks Estella up after our meetings. Ernie also comes to our occasional lunchtime feasts. I don't know where he hatched the phrase,***
***"Don't talk to me about gherkins!"***
***I couldn't resist trying to write a poem about that. It's a strange word, gherkins, and it truly does only have two possible rhymes; firkin and mirkin. Find out about Ernie, gherkins, firkins and mirkins right here.***

12th July, 2016

There's a wise old man called Ernie,
who lives down by the Maylandsea shore,
He's been growing a beard to hide his face,
For fifty years or more.
I think he's an octogenarian,
perhaps he's The old man of the sea,
I think he harbours a secret,
He's concealing from you and from me.
I asked him once what his secret was,
to keeping his old heart working,
He looked at me through his wise old eyes, and said,
"Don't talk to me about gherkins."

Ernie will talk to you about anything you like,
About politics, religion and sex,
He'll argue with you 'til you're black and blue,
And get you all heated and vexed.
He'll talk about the sky, and apple pies and D.I.Y.
And natter on about any matter you don't understand,
He'll waffle and procrastinate, pontificate and quietly debate,
On any subject that accidentally comes to hand.
His knowledge is as long as his beard,
And his beard would rival Rasputin's
But he draws the line and calls time by saying,
"Don't talk to me about gherkins."

Ernie was hungry and went down to the chippie
To buy a ton of chips and a wing of skate,
He'd been working hard in the garden all day,
And he wasn't pleased to have to wait.
His hunger grew as he stood in the queue,
His appetite came in on a trolley,
He asked the lovely chip shop girl,
"Could you throw me in a wally?"
She said "Sorry ain't got none of them."
He said, "Really! What's in that big jar a-lurking?"
She said, "Oh them are pickled cucumbers."
He said, "Don't talk to me about gherkins."

Research for this poem didn't come easy, that's for sure,
But after all, that's what I've got a rhyming dictionary for,
There are really only two words
that have a perfect rhyme with gherkin
First, there's an old fashioned measure of liquid
that once was called a firkin,
And last there's an interesting word
I'd never heard of before,
it's something called a merkin.

It's a device to hide your modesty
like Adam and Eve's leaves of figs,
A merkin my dears,
Now I know you are all ears,
Is a decorative pubic wig.
So merkin, firkin, gherkin, and that's your lot,
I'm really sad to have to tell,
Please don't talk to me about hairy merkins,
And it would be best to avoid discussion
about firkin gherkins as well.

Ernie's seen a lot of changes over the years,
The world keeps spinning and none of us will last
One thing that's definitely not good,
Is the emergence of food that's fast.
Ronald McDonald lives everywhere,
from rising moon to setting sun,
And nobody knows why his big macs

have a gherkin in the burger bun.

I think it would be very apt and not absurd,
When Ernie croaks and has his last laugh
That he have carved on his gravestone in bold letters,
"Don't talk to me about gherkins."
Yes! That's his epitaph.

The Fall

**Well look! Here we are in September, and what's happening to the weather? In 2016 I'm pretty sure that Autumn arrived with a bang.**

September 2016

Once again another month quick disappears,
and nights draw in to warn of dying summer days,
while autumn colours invade to shade the lands.
Then it won't be long before the daylight becomes curtailed,
and winds are blowing bold and colder under
the growing shadows of winter's chilling hands.

Perhaps now we can all understand
why they call the end of Summer the Fall,
As the shadow of a sudden shuddering hand
turns a tight grip on us all.
But the way it arrived in a few hours overnight
with a smash and grab so brash,
I'm surprised that we phrase it as the Fall at all,
when it's been nearer to a crash!"

Stardust (Nicole's Song)

***My life changed in Autumn 2016 when I met a new partner. The name of this lovely lady is Nicole. She is a geologist. We discussed what really happens when we leave this world. Perhaps it is typical from a geological point of view that, "We become stardust". To a geologist, that is where everything came from, and where everything will go back to. We are and always will be infinitesimally small and insignificant in the context of time and space.***
***I've had a comment from someone I know that the lyric to the "Let us fly..." bit of this song is almost Shakespearean. As a poet and writer that is a compliment indeed.***
***Nicole translated the words of that bit of the song into something similar in French. Makes it sound very posh indeed.***
***The song was recorded on the CD album "And the Band Played On" at Highfield Studios in November 2015.***

27th October, 2016 to 17th November, 2016

Let us fly to the heart of the stars
and be lost in the dust of endless time,
for we are but moments in the fullness of ages,
a fleeting brush with sweet echoes of love.

We will walk long sandy shores of an ocean of sweet dreams,
and be found in the sounds of crashing waves,
For we are but a smile in the trail of the stars,
a stolen kiss from the lips of our Earth.

We've heard music in mountains singing songs to the heavens,
in the glacier and volcano we've seen ice and seen fire,
but we become humbled in the smallness of our being,
and can only stand and wonder at awesome power.

Let us fly to the heart of the stars
and be lost in the dust of endless time,
for we are but moments in the fullness of ages,
a fleeting brush with sweet echoes of love.

In the cold eye of a storm we have heard whispering winds
We've counted every grain of sand on our small beach,
But we're silenced in amazement at how many stars fill the Universe,
And far too many answers are still out of reach.

Let us fly to the heart of the stars
and be lost in the dust of endless time,
for we are but moments in the fullness of ages,
a fleeting brush with sweet echoes of love.

"Allons voler au coeur des etoiles,
et perdons nous dans le temps sans fin,
car nous sommes qu'instants dans la plenitude du temp,
une caresse fugace aux echos tendres d'amour."

Zebra in t' Chippie

***A colleague at the Maldon Writer's Group brought along a picture of a zebra standing in a chip shop. She said that it was absolutely for real, and she had seen it first hand on a holiday in Yorkshire.***
***I couldn't resist trying to write a poem that fits the scenario, (With a Yorkshire accent of course).***

17th/19th November, 2016

I were walkin ' ome from t' Orse and 'Ounds;
it were a lovely bright, moonlight night.
I'd only 'ad 6 or 7 pints of best bitter,
and I were feelin' quite alright.

I wandered down t' Igh Street,
swaying this way and that,
feelin' like I didn't ave a care in t' world,
Must 'ave looked a right lairy prat.

And then my eyes went out on stalks,
and I couldn't believe what I'd seen,
across t 'road in t' moonlight,
there it was staring back at me.

There were a zebra in t' Chippie,
standin' upright bold as brass,
black and white stripes all up his legs,
and disappearing up his arse.

He stood there so proud and strong,
on those long striped pyjama legs,
'E wasn't doin' out that was wrong,
but 'is snout were in t' pickled eggs.

But t'chippie were closed up for t' night,
and I couldn't go in there to find,
why were a zebra a-standin' there,
Mindin' 'is own business mind.

I went 'ome feelin' most perplexed,
you know, I thought I was seein' things,
the sort of hallucinations that,
a night out on t' beer may bring.

Well, nevertheless I slept like a log,
And woke up in t' fire,
In t' mornin' me brain were still abuzz,
from what had recently transpired.

A zebra in t' chippie,
I ask yer 'ow can that be right,
It's not the sort of thing yer expect to see,
On a lovely moonlit night.

So when the lunchtime came around next day,
I'd 'ave chips and a wing of skate,
down in t' chippie that afternoon,
before the hour got too late.

I resolved to solve my riddle there and then,
There were questions I needed to answer,
why in the world were there a zebra in t' chippie,
munching away on the pickled eggs,
the stripy legged prancer.

The sign outside said fish and chips,
It were clear what the man were sellin',
I stood outside with me mouth salivatin',
from the aromas I was smellin'.

Then I went inside and joined t' queue,
as we shuffled towards t'  till,
and then I asked to see the boss,
I think 'is name were Bill.

'E came out front in 'is straw 'at
and greeted me wi' a smile, and said
"What can I do for thee then lad?"
in his confident fishmonger style.

"Eee! I just wanted to know something,
I've a question that's mighty queer.
I walked past 'ere late last night,
and there was a zebra standin' 'ere."

Now Bill he pulled me quietly aside,
and said, "Aye lad, there is good reason,
You see fish stocks are dwindlin' fast on t' Dogger bank,
especially in this season.

And I can't see it improvin' soon,
what wi' stingy EU quotas,
our fishing industry's all but dead,
killed by bureaucratic Brussels voters.

The Russians send their factory ships,
the French and Spanish steal the rest,
while we scrape along doing nothing wrong,
still tryin' t' do our level best."

"So although I know it says Fish and Chips
on t' sign above the door,
I'm afraid to say that the time 'as come,
that were selling fish no more.

You see, lad, we've 'ad to diversify,
Or take t' business to t' wall,
We've got 'ungry customers t' satisfy,
They still want their hot grub and all.

So I've been out on t' safari in Africa,
On t' Serengeti plains in t' sizzling 'eat,
And made a deal with tribesman there,
to supply me wi' fresh meat."

That zebra that yer saw last night,
'As been t' t' butcher's 'ook,
'E's in t' back all ground to mince,
I'll show thee if yer want to 'ave a look.

I'm putting 'im on as t' special this week.
I'm doin' stripy sausages and burgers yer see,
and you could say they're sellin' like 'ot cakes,
would you want one for yer tea?

"Well, no," I said, "I came 'ere for skate and chips."
Again I were feelin' quite vexed,
"OK!" he said, "Come back next week,
we're tryin' out wildebeest patties next."

## Aldeburgh Days - 1 and 2

***In December 2016 my partner, Nicole, and I stayed at the Wentworth Hotel in Aldeburgh on the Suffolk coast for a few days, and I wrote these poems after we returned home.***

8th December, 2016

Shingle shifted underfoot,
pebbles rhythm called the waves,
the swell was wild in constant rage
we walked there hand in hand,
just us, you and me.

The scallop stood, so proud and strong,
I hear those voices that will not be drowned
we stopped and kissed under the shell,
our smiles and eyes were meeting there,
alone next to the sea.

A cold North Sea in winter days,
sweeping along the strand in cruel pain,
never ever can hope to undermine,
the steadfast defiance of such lonely hearts.
together in harmony.

9th December, 2016

Windows tall and wide in breakfast rooms;
looking out,
over fishing shacks and shingle beach
towards tall skies emptied of clouds.

Morning sun, golden on the horizon;
rising up,
burns a brilliant mirror on the sea
heralds a day made for you and me.

Southwold Day - part 1

***While staying inn Aldeburgh we visited the lovely seaside resort of Southwold, lovely even in Winter blowing a gale. Again, I wrote this poem after we returned home.***

14th December, 2016

Along the strand northwards we're driving,
through Thorpness,
past the Meare,
where Peter Pan once played,
and admiring,
the House in the Clouds,
once a water tower,
and on inland.

There's the Parrot and Punchbowl,
pink and perfect;
since 1576?
A crossroads in Leiston town,
and we turn towards the East,
along King George's Avenue.

Soon we find something interesting,
off road,
in the fields.
Leiston Abbey,
beautiful monastic ruin,
old Henry 8 done it again,
with his dissolution quest.
Premonstratensian edifice,
Ranulf de Glanville, 1182.

A worthy stroll,
clambering round and over
old walls and brickwork,
and a good look reveals
a magnificent Tudor house,
little doors,
ball-pane windows.

Entered through
an octagonal brick turret,
saw the cellarer’s range,
the warming house and dorter,
fine chequer work in flint,
rocks and stones,
excitement!

This is right up your street.
I'm happy,
you're happy.
Job done.

# CHAPTER 9

## Xenophobia

***"It was 1877 when xenophobia first appeared,
and it amused me when I found out
that bulldozer and Mexican stand-off arrived,
in the very same year."***

Last Day in Aldeburgh

***Still with the memories of Aldeburgh flooding my mind, and already nearly 2 months later, this poem arrived.***

30th January, 2017

Awake in the Wentworth Hotel;
the last morning of our stay,
Breakfast and then a slow stroll,
along the High Street way.

Down to the craft butcher shop;
the premises of Salter and King,
to buy a locally reared leg of lamb,
for weekend roast dinner enjoying.

Then pack, check out and pay the bill;
homeward bound on a sunny day
gliding through the Suffolk fields,
heading Woodbridge way.

Anticipate a pretty place
to stop and have a look around,
try as we might - no place to park,
so again we are southward bound.

Destination Ipswich harbour,
A port since Saxon days,
on a bend in the River Orwell,
loop the loop to find the place.

On the harbour, waterfront,
once a dock that served to export wool,
built in the reign of Edward the third,
when Gipeswic it was called.

Lunch in the Grazing Sheep upstairs,
quiche and salad, me and you,
holding hands across the table
admiring the lovely view.

A walk along the quayside,
in the mid-afternoon sunshine sky,
past the Custom House and Isaac Lord's,
we talk, admire and walk on by.

Marina, luxury yachts, and dredger ships,
equipped for harbour and sea,
towards a black and white building
like a giant chess board,
Suffolk University.
A place that has a fine slogan,
displayed for all to see,
"It's never too late to become the person
you always wanted to be."

And what have we become today,
after our beautiful Wentworth stay?
We've enjoyed good times together,
become closer to each other I'd say,
I wouldn't have missed it for the world,
remember our Aldeburgh days.

Recording and Compilation of CD album "Angel's Rainbow"

***This album was recorded at Highfield Studios to coincide with the publication of my novel "Angel's Rainbow". This eclectic collection of songs and music includes an instrumental, songs arising from old lyrics, a brand new song, "Stardust", and songs previously recorded on past albums.***

May 23rd 2017

| Chord | Key | Capo | Title | Recorded |
|---|---|---|---|---|
| Emin | Emin | 0 | BEGIN (Instrumental) | 23/05/17 |
| Amin | Amin | 0 | Going in Search of Angels | 23/05/17 |
| Gmaj | Gmaj | 0 | Promises and Regrets | 23/05/17 |
| Gmaj | Amaj | 2 | Separate Heavens | 16/11/05 |
| Amin | Amin | 0 | Only Turning Over Stones (Meet the Spirit) | 9/2000 |
| Emaj | Emaj | 0 | Dangerous Curves | 01/06/15 |
| Amin | Cmin | 3 | Don't you wonder? | 24/09/03 |
| Gmaj | Gmaj | 0 | The Horizon | 23/05/17 |
| Gmaj | Bbmaj | 3 | All you can become | 24/09/03 |
| Cmaj | Dmaj | 2 | Everlasting Light | 22/07/02 |
| Cmaj | Cmaj | 0 | Armistice | 01/2000 |
| Emin | F#min | 2 | Clear September Sky – part 2 - the Answer | 24/09/03 |
| Emin | F#min | 2 | Clear September Sky - part 1 - Question | 24/09/03 |
| Emin | Emin | 0 | And the band played on | 11/15 |
| Dmaj | Dmaj | 0 | Stardust | 23/05/17 |

## Melancholy Premonitions, Spooky Omens and Superstitions

***This poem came together for a homework exercise from the Maldon Writer's Group. I researched superstitions with my friend Mr Google and then collated a few sometimes very odd ones together. So, perhaps it doesn't make any sense, but who cares. It's just a construction of poetic fun.***

10th July, 2017

I searched my spooky omens
and melancholy premonitions,
And took a step back from the edge
and made a quick decision.

I'd curtail my silly superstitions
while I stopped not tempting fate,
but then I touched wood and crossed
my fingers before it got too late.

I've been opening umbrellas indoors
but have never cut my toenails after dark you see,
I've walked under every ladder
I've seen clutching a rabbit's foot to protect me

I've made many a wish upon a wishbone,
and stared in the face with an evil eye,
and if a black cat dares to cross my path,
I'll pause and let it walk on by.

Those black cats and black birds that haunt,
are for witches and Halloween,
Ravens made foretell of doom,
who cares if they were born on Friday 13.

I've broken mirrors often not liking what I see,
but if I find a penny, I'll pick it up,
I'll always smile at single magpies,
but I'm still a believer in beginner's luck.

So they say that bad luck always comes in threes,
so I turn around three times and say,
If 666 is the number of the beast,
well the devil and me can ride out together today.

I won't knock on wood for a safe connection
to salvation or divinity,
And smashing another mirror
won't bring seven years bad luck for me.

I've been to Germany many times
and toasted my friends not with beer but water,
In Argentina I was born the seventh son,
the spawn of the devil's daughter.

I've been to Norway on my travels,
and I've whistled indoors and it didn't rain,
Then birds have flown into my home,
and haven't caused me death or pain.

You can bless me when I sneeze,
and sing ring a ring a roses,
I'm not going to fall down and die,
I'll avoid what the atishoo proposes.

NOTES:

Friday 13th, Jesus died on Good Friday,
in Spain it's Tuesday 13th, Martes,
Roman God of War = violence, death and bloodshed
whistling indoors in Russia = financial problems
Sit at the corner of a table and you will never marry
lay a purse or wallet on the ground = bad financial luck.

## Brick walls

***A piece of writing that was supposed to be about brick walls, but I used poetic license and lateral thinking to turn it into a political diatribe. It was election time and the Brexit fiasco was in full flow so why not. I come back to bricks at the end with an easy solution to all our political problems. Not really! My tongue is firmly in my cheek.***

12th July, 2017

Bricks red regular angles, oblong and uniform in shape
Gathered patterns pulled together barriers to make
Enclose, protect, imprison, guard
strong and stubborn cruel and hard.

A brick in hand a building block
or poised to be a weapon, for attack
Bricks mortared together in a wall,
Defence!
Brick walls to hold you back.
But behind these walls there's subterfuge,
cunning, deceit and lies,
where politicians cling tight to their truths
and feed us lullabies.

Hoorah! So once again we get the chance
to vote for a smooth path to our future,
it's strong and stable leadership on one side
and a coalition of chaos on the other.
Can you say which way will suit you?

With promises like water lapping around me,
I stood on the flood plain of possibilities,
and on the far bank a runaway train of propaganda
steamed by at mighty speed.
The train came to a shaky bridge
that crossed a yawning chasm
Separating me from tomorrow,
and all my past from a future

Was there ever any safe place
to seek refuge or sanctuary?
because out in the big brave world
conflict reigns supreme.
as the North Korean stupid boy shakes his rattle
and threatens nuclear war,
while a ginger-blonde twat called Donald
tells us that climate change is just a myth.

They tell us everything will be all right
and Brexit will turn out fine;
Vote for me and you'll soon see how strong we all will be.
Vote for him and the chances are slim
that we'll survive his red faced Marxist fate.
Vote now for us, jump on our beautiful blue bus,
before it gets too late.

Corbyn nationalizes utilities and saves the NHS
from a slow and certain death,
May takes pensioner's rights away
and gives huge pay rises to her fat cat mates.
And oh Nicola! The poisoned dwarf,
the spawn of Jimmy Crankie drones and spins,
all about the UK getting out
while her bonnie Scotland stays in.

But overnight strong and stable turned
and quickly became weak and wobbly,
so now we're up shit creek again
and the fat cat Brussels bureaucrats
laugh their heads off and rub their hands with glee.
while we head for yet another constitutional crisis
brought about by democracy?

So here we have a midsummer madness
at the height of flaming June,
so we can watch all out politicians

throwing snowballs at the moon.
Who said we are going to build a better world
that's safe for everyone, trust me and you'll see?
It's such a wonderful scheme, a realizable dream,
and we call it democracy.

Well, Corbyn didn't win, but he smiles inanely
and claims a victory anyway,
And May shot herself in the foot and finds herself
standing on the thinnest ice,
Nicola got a bloody nose
for her persistent referendum requests, Nice!

And the political terrorists at the DUP
were the gang that came off best,
Goodbye UKip, hard luck to the Greens,
and the Libdems in limbo land
everybody lost, nobody won,
together we fall, disunited we stand.

I've an idea to solve all the problems,
and it's radicalism rotten
Let's build a brick wall, line them all up against it,
and shoot the bloody lot of 'em.

Keeping A Diary

***Sometimes there's a need to ignore the title and subject matter completely because perhaps there something else on my mind that needs to be brought to life. This writing exercise was one of those occasions. Once again it's just a bit of fun with the wonder of words and the English language.***

10th August, 2017

So, there's a task I've been asked to undertake
to make sense of keeping a diary.
But the words won't come easily.
So I'll have to fudge the issue in hand
by writing around a theme.
And then edging my way towards a conclusion
that is satisfactory.

Perhaps it's a bit like starting off
the construction of a jigsaw puzzle,
by first finding and fixing all the edges of the frame.
Once that has been achieved
I can start to fill in the void in the middle
by gradually
building an image to complete the game

But I've been trapped inside tall prison walls
for many days on end,
going round and round in a weird word maze
while my great pretender friend,
madam inspiration
has deserted me and moved to another place.
Perhaps she is hitch-hiking her way
across the wild blue yonder
or falling fast through space?

I remember how
the elusive muse used to come flowing through
like rainbows in warm sunshine and wet rain.
But when writer's block arrives and locks

my words inside my brain again
I feel I must break out and find out quick
how to click the switch to go for write, write, write
because when there's work to be done,
 well, it ain't no fun
to be gripped and choked in this vice so tight.

to record when keeping a diary is the quest.
Sure thing, it's tough job, but someone's gotta do it,
so I'll do my best,
as I ought.
But. Hey listen! there's not a lot of difference
between memorize and mesmerize
Just a crazy little snake that hisses "Eeeee" not "Oh",
and settles in the midst of my random thoughts.

Or shall I abandon this daft idea?
I know, I'll write about keeping a dairy instead.
It's just the "Eye" and the "Ay"
that have danced around,
while the "Dee" and the "Are"
and the "Why" are still found.
So, from dates and times and events
I've been ever so slightly overhauled,
and on the way they've been replaced
by udders and moos and milking stools

Well beauty is in "Eye" of the beholder,
and we're told to make "Ay" while the sun shines,
while Tweedledum and Tweedledee just "Are"
and have no need to wonder "Why?"
And that's it for now my writing friends,
my muse, is at an end again.
So I'll bid you all farewell.
Goodbye!

## Xenophobia

***Subject matter for homework at a writer's group is occasionally based on someone's mistaken perception of a situation between two people. That's how this came about, but I had to use it in my own way to take a humorous look at some phobias.***

16th November, 2017

Many years ago,
on the shores of the Mediterranean Sea,
some very wise and learned men
defined some words for me.
So looking back to ancient Greece
we could come to a conclusion,
that it was fun to play with words,
and make literal confusion.

When they linked up the word xenos,
which means a guest or stranger
with another word, phobos
named after the fear of war.
Then that became a new word,
and we knew what it was for.
Its origins therefore defined,
in the late 19th century,
and that was how I'll tell you,
xenophobia came to be.
It was 1877 when xenophobia first appeared,
and it amused me when I found out
that bulldozer and Mexican stand-off arrived,
in the very same year.

Now that we had a word for it, it wouldn't be too long
before we could have a fear of strangers and foreigners
and all the things that they do wrong.
Xenophobia therefore is a fear and hatred
of strangers or foreigners
or of anything that is foreign or strange,
a fear of the unknown, you know,

xenos and phobia rearranged.

But that's enough of this demented ramble,
a sufficient definition it is clear,
my research has turned up more interesting things,
that relate to our phobias and fears.
Whilst your xenophobia is fine by me,
you've got to fear something, it's true,
be proud, and British, and suspicious,
be true to yourself, that will do.

But did you know all these things I will say
just to educate and amuse you?

The fear of fear, or the thought of being
afraid of objects or situations
now that is Phobophobia.
The fear of everything or fear that
terrible things will happen
Is known as Panophobia.
The fear of opinions, or being afraid
of hearing what others are thinking of you
now that is Allodoxaphobia.
If you have a fear of the future,
or a persistent fear of what is to come
you are suffering from Chronophobia.
Perhaps you could be forgiven because after all that
you may have a fear of the definition of phobias.

Here's a strange one, because it's possible
that it really doesn't exist,
Homophobia, which is a fear of homosexuality,
doesn't appear in all lists.

The fear of getting old is very common,
although ageing is the most natural thing to do.
Gerascophobia is it's name,
and it will happen to me and you.

The fear of technology apparently,
is often induced by religion or culture,
and perhaps by age.
They call it Technophobia,
not defined by a Grecian sage.

Let's have a bit of fun with words,
and define our very own phobia.
If you are old and fear technology,
do you have Gerascotechnophobia?

In all seriousness now let's carry on,
in a lighter hearted vein,
If you have a fear of fat people,
Cacomorphobia is to blame.

I know you will really like this last phobia,
that I intend to inflict upon you,
Well, Hippo poto monstro sesquippedalio phobia,
Is a fear of long words,
And believe it or not, it’s true.

Ode to Chelmsford (Gridlocked)

***When I lived in a village called Sandon just a few miles outside Chelmsford there was a wonderful Park and Ride bus service which could whisk you into town in about 5 minutes. It was all the more wonderful because I could walk to the terminal in 10 minutes and travel for free with my senior citizen bus pass. Free travel into town!***
***You don't get much for free in this day and age.***
***However, if you travelled back home after about 4 in the afternoon then it was no longer wonderful. Traffic build up in Chelmsford, particularly along Parkway and approaching the widely renowned Army and Navy roundabout, caused frustratingly time consuming delays.***
***The original inspiration for these song lyrics came about while sitting in gridlocked traffic on the Park and Ride bus. I recall it took over 40 minutes to get home.***
***The song was recorded for me by my great friend Ralph Orme and I had the opportunity to perform it at the Cramphorn Theatre in Chelmsford. There are several different versions, but here I've only included the original*** **"Ode to Chelmsford (Gridlocked)" and a generic version which could apply to any gridlocked town. God knows there are plenty of them. !It was an immense pleasure and privilege to perform the original at the Cramphorn Theatre in Chelmsford, and to have the performance extremely well received.**

29th December, 2017

Gather around me all my friends
and listen to the tale I tell,
of hold ups in our city streets
and potholes big as hell;
of grief and strife and biting nails,
frustration without end,
a problem most insoluble,
cause the town's gridlocked again.

The Army and Navy flyover was built,
as a single lane tidal flow,
it's always open in the opposite direction,
to the way I want to go,
and the council put up traffic lights,
that drive you round the bend,
on every busy roundabout,
so we're all gridlocked again.

Oh the town's gridlocked again,
and I just don't know when,
when I'll reach my destination,
'cause the town's gridlocked again.

So, is it so good that we're a city now,
and prices have gone sky high?
They're building here, and building there,
and building in the sky.
An influx of Bond Street four by fours,
seems to be a growing trend,
but now the car parks are all chock-a-block,
and the town's gridlocked again.

And you'll pay a King's ransom to park in town,
that is if you ever arrive.
In our fair town of Chelmsford it's understood,
you're in for a slow, slow drive.
Springfield Road and Broomfield Road,
and Parkway get one out of ten.
Perhaps it's mission impossible,
because the town's gridlocked again.

Oh the town's gridlocked again,
and I just don't know when,
when I'll reach my destination,
'cause the town's gridlocked again.

I was on my way to Cote Brasserie,
for a Frenchie romantic dinner.
Just my lady, a bottle of wine and me,
seemed I was on to a winner.

But I got held up by heavy traffic,
and arrived at ten past ten,
She thought that I had stood her up,
but the town was gridlocked again.

Oh dear! There'd been an accident,
and how did it come about?
Why it's mister selfish on his mobile;
I wish he'd leave it out.
He's brought my town to a standstill again,
because he couldn't wait to text,
and his utter rank stupidity means,
that the town's gridlocked again.

Oh the town's gridlocked again,
and I just don't know when,
when I'll reach my destination,
'cause the town's gridlocked again.

I was on the Baddow bypass yesterday,
waiting in the usual queue
of traffic stacked back over a mile,
and I wasn't sure what I could do,
except twiddle my thumbs and scratch my bum,
until the bitter end,
'cause I wasn't going anywhere,
while the town was gridlocked again.

When I finally made it on to Parkway,
I was feeling pretty sick.
I was supposed to be at the cinema,
to enjoy the latest flick
After hours and hours standing still
the film was over. Amen!
Oh praise the Lord Almighty God,
'cause the town's gridlocked again.

Oh the town's gridlocked again,
and I just don't know when,
when I'll reach my destination,
'cause the town's gridlocked again.

If I take a trip to Brentwood or Maldon,
or Lakeside shopping park,
Basildon or Colchester,
would surely make the mark.
They keep the traffic flowing there,
or that's what they intend.
But it's a certainty in Chelmsford,
that the town's gridlocked again.

I'd consider a move to Yorkshire,
somewhere in the Moors or Dales.
I'll spruce up the house all nice and posh,
and put it up for sale.
If I get my happy motoring there,
I'll be able to pretend,
that I don't give a monkey's anymore,
when the town's gridlocked again.

Oh the town's gridlocked again,
and I just don't know when,
when I'll reach my destination,
'cause the town's gridlocked again.

So, if you want to spend a lifetime,
frustrated in a steaming queue,
staring hard into the great grey yonder,
breathing traffic fumes,
then join our city's biggest club,
get in your car, and then,
you'll be tearing out your hair because,
the town's gridlocked again.

Oh the town's gridlocked again,
and I just don't know when,
when I'll reach my destination,
'cause the town's gridlocked again.

The Gridlocked Song: Generic Version

**So here is the generic version of the "Ode to Chelmsford (Gridlocked)"**
**Does it apply to your town or city?**
**More than likely.**

Original 29th December, 2017, adapted version 15th February, 2018

Gather around me all my friends
and listen to the tale I tell,
of hold ups in our busy streets
and potholes big as hell;
of grief and strife and biting nails,
frustration without end,
a problem most insoluble,
cause the town's gridlocked again.

Oh the town's gridlocked again,
and I just don't know when,
I'll reach my destination,
'cause the town's gridlocked again.

I was on my way into town today,
waiting in the usual queue
of traffic stacked back over a mile,
and I wasn't sure what I could do,
except twiddle my thumbs and scratch my bum,
until the bitter end,
'cause I wasn't going anywhere,
while the town's was gridlocked again.

Oh the town's gridlocked again
and I just don't know when,
I'll reach my destination,
'cause the town's gridlocked again.

When I finally made it into the town centre
I was feeling pretty sick.
I was supposed to be at the cinema,

to enjoy the latest flick
After hours and hours standing still,
the film was over. Amen!
Oh praise the Lord Almighty God,
'cause the town's gridlocked again.

Oh the town's gridlocked again,
and I just don't know when,
I'll reach my destination,
'cause the town's gridlocked again.

If you look at the way things are heading now,
with prices going sky high?
When they're building here, and building there,
and building in the sky.
An influx of badly driven four by fours,
seems to be a growing trend,
so the car parks are all chock-a-block,
and the town's gridlocked again.

Oh the town's gridlocked again,
and I just don't know when,
I'll reach my destination,
'cause the town's gridlocked again.

So the council put up traffic lights,
that will drive you to distraction,
Mini- roundabouts and one-way streets,
can't get no satisfaction,
They say it keeps the traffic flowing,
and if that's what they intend.
Why is it a stone cold certainty
that the town's gridlocked again.

Oh the town's gridlocked again,
and I just don't know when,
I'll reach my destination
'cause the town's gridlocked again.

You'll pay a King's ransom to park in town,
that is if you ever arrive.
In my fair town it is understood,
I'm in for a slow, slow drive?
Take any road in town anytime,
and I'd give it one out of ten.
Perhaps it's mission impossible,
because the town's gridlocked again.

Oh the town's gridlocked again,
and I just don't know when,
I'll reach my destination
'cause the town's gridlocked again.

I was on my way to a restaurant,
for a Frenchie romantic dinner.
Just my lady, a bottle of wine and me,
seemed I was on to a winner.
But I got held up by heavy traffic,
and arrived at ten past ten,
She thought that I had stood her up,
but the town's was gridlocked again.

Oh the town's gridlocked again,
and I just don't know when,
I'll reach my destination,
'cause the town's gridlocked again.

Oh dear! There'd been an accident,
and how did it come about?
Why, it's mister selfish on his mobile;
I wish he'd leave it out.
He's brought the town's to a standstill again,
because he couldn't wait to text,
and his utter rank stupidity means,
that the town's gridlocked again.

Oh the town's gridlocked again,
and I just don't know when,
I'll reach my destination,
'cause the town's gridlocked again.

I'd consider a move to Yorkshire,
somewhere in the Moors or Dales.
I'll spruce up the house all nice and posh,
and put it up for sale.
If I get my happy motoring there,
I'll be able to pretend,
that I don't give a monkey's anymore,
when the town's gridlocked again.

Oh the town's gridlocked again,
and I just don't know when,
I'll reach my destination,
'cause the town's gridlocked again.

So, if you want to spend a lifetime,
frustrated in a steaming queue,
staring hard into the great grey yonder,
breathing traffic fumes,
then join your town's biggest club,
get in your car, and then,
you'll be tearing out your hair because,
the town's gridlocked again.

Oh the town's gridlocked again,
and I just don't know when,
I'll reach my destination,
'cause the town's gridlocked again.

Other Titles by Michael Haley
Published in Great Britain by Mirador Publishing

Chelmsford 2012 - Many Hearts - One Mind
ISBN 978-1-910104-76-7 (Novel - Humour)

First City of Essex - Many Diversions One Destination
ISBN 978-1-910530-04-7 (Novel - Humour)

An Idea Appeared
ISBN 978-1-910330-64-1 (Poetry)

Turning Over Stones
ISBN: 978-1-911044-46-8
(Poems, Song Lyrics, Stories and Recording History)

Angel's Rainbow
ISBN 978-1-912192-44-1 (Novel - Inspirational)

A Little Collection of Short Stories
ISBN: 978-1-913264-17-8 (Stories and Poems)

Tall Words on a Wall
ISBN: 978-1-913833-10-7
(Poems, Song Lyrics, Stories and Recording History)

The Old Dog and Duck Chronicles (Short Novel - Humour)
ISBN:978-1-914965-10-4

Tangles, Twists and Turns (Novel - Whodunnit)
ISBN:978-1-914965-69-2

First Published in Great Britain 2023 by Mirador Publishing



First edition: 2023



A copy of this work is available through the British Library.

ISBN: 978-1-915953-06-3

Mirador Publishing
10 Greenbrook Terrace
Taunton
Somerset
UK
TA1 1UT

Printed in Great Britain
by Amazon

23151823R00148